Berlin Travel Guide

Captivating Adventures through a Historic Wall Trail, Vibrant Street Art, Landmarks, Hidden Gems, and More

Welcome Aboard, Discover Your Limited-Time Free Bonus!

Hello, traveler! Welcome to the Captivating Travels family, and thanks for grabbing a copy of this book! Since you've chosen to join us on this journey, we'd like to offer you something special.

Check out the link below for a **FREE** Ultimate Travel Checklist eBook & Printable PDF to make your travel planning stress-free and enjoyable.

But that's not all - you'll also gain access to our exclusive email list with even more free e-books and insider travel tips. Well, what are you waiting for? Click the link below to join and embark on your next adventure with ease.

Access your bonus here:
https://livetolearn.lpages.co/checklist/
Or, Scan the QR code!

Table of Contents

Introduction

Forget the guidebooks that weigh you down and the online tips that leave you lost!

Prepare to stroll through Berlin, not as a tourist, but as a local. You'll be effortlessly navigating cobbled lanes, savoring authentic flavors, and unearthing hidden gems. No more deciphering cryptic maps or scrambling for last-minute translations. This book is your friendly companion, explicitly written for first-time visitors to Berlin.

The map below shows the areas covered in this book. The numbers indicate the chapter numbers.

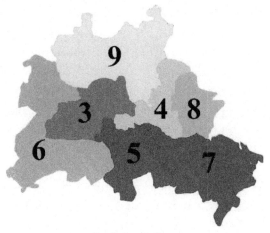

Berlin by chapter.

Clear instructions, practical tips, and actionable itineraries guide you through every step, from navigating the airport to uncovering Berlin's vibrant soul. However, this isn't just a "how-to" manual. Each chapter explores a distinct district, inviting you to experience the city's diverse offerings.

Chapter 1: Get to Know Berlin lays the foundation, introducing you to the city's history, culture, and one-of-a-kind quirks. You'll understand the rhythm of Berlin, from its buzzing nightlife to its serene parks.

Chapter 2: To and From the Airport ensures a smooth transition, with detailed instructions on navigating public transportation, taxis, and rideshares. No more frantic arrivals or stressful departures.

Chapter 3: Mitte - Charlottenburg-Wilmersdorf takes you to the heart of Berlin, where iconic landmarks like the Brandenburg Gate and Reichstag stand tall. You'll explore elegant palaces, discover hidden courtyards, and savor the best currywurst in town.

Chapter 4: Kreuzberg-Friedrichshain - Lichtenberg plunges you into the city's gritty underbelly, where street art explodes on every wall, and nightlife pulsates in hidden clubs. You'll discover the remnants of the Berlin Wall, vibrant Turkish markets, and a youthful energy that defies definition.

Chapter 5: Neukölln - Tempelhof-Schöneberg reveals a kaleidoscope of cultures, from hipster cafes to immigrant communities. You'll find vintage treasures, sample international cuisines, and witness the city's artistic spirit in galleries and street performances.

Chapter 6: Steglitz-Zehlendorf - Spandau provides a glimpse into Berlin's calmer side, with sprawling parks, tranquil lakes, and family-friendly attractions. You'll escape the urban bustle, explore historic palaces, and discover hidden gems like the Botanical Garden.

Chapter 7: Treptow - Köpenick takes you to the banks of the Spree River, where nature meets history. You'll stroll through serene parks, visit the Soviet War Memorial, and discover the charming island of Köpenick, with its quirky museums and boat tours.

Chapter 8: Marzahn-Hellersdorf ventures beyond the tourist trail, revealing a district in flux, where modern architecture blends with socialist remnants. You'll see the city's changing face, explore street art projects, and discover a local perspective on Berlin's future.

Chapter 9: <u>Pankow – Reinickendorf</u> offers a breath of fresh air with vast green spaces, charming neighborhoods, and a laid-back atmosphere. You'll visit the Mauerpark flea market, explore the historic Pankow district, and discover hidden lakes perfect for a picnic.

Chapter 10: <u>City Itineraries and Programs</u> provides curated plans for different interests and durations, from art lovers to history buffs and foodies to budget travelers. You can choose your adventure, maximizing your time and experiencing the city like a true Berliner.

Chapter 11: <u>Day Trips Beyond the City</u> expands your horizons to nearby Potsdam with its stunning palaces or Sachsenhausen concentration camp, a poignant reminder of the past.

Bonus Chapter: <u>Useful German Survival Phrases</u> – this handy bonus equips you with essential words and expressions to navigate basic situations confidently. Order your currywurst like a pro, ask for directions, and greet the locals with a friendly "Guten Tag."

Berlin Travel Guide is more than just a book. It's your key to unlocking an unforgettable Berlin experience. Regardless of your interests or travel style, this guide will empower you to discover the city's hidden gems, connect with its vibrant soul, and create memories that last a lifetime.

Chapter 1: Get to Know Berlin

Stroll down Berlin's cobbled streets, and you'll be swept into a captivating mixture of past and present. Grand avenues lined with Prussian-era architecture speak tales of emperors and revolutions. Trendy street art and bustling cafes pulsate with dynamic, modern metropolis energy. Berlin is a living, breathing testament to resilience, reinvention, and a relentless pursuit of artistic and cultural expression. From the somber Berlin Wall to the electrifying beat of techno clubs, prepare to be captivated by a city where history emerges from every corner and the future explodes in every color.

Map of Berlin.
No machine-readable author provided. Puregenius assumed (based on copyright claims). CC BY-SA 2.5 <https://creativecommons.org/licenses/by-sa/2.5>, via Wikimedia Commons.
https://commons.wikimedia.org/wiki/File:Berlin_friedrichshain-kreuzberg.png

Berlin: A City Etched by History

Berlin's story is a thrilling epic, etched in stone and graffiti, smiles and roars. The city has always been a crucible of change, from its humble beginnings as a medieval trading post to its modern incarnation as a cultural and economic powerhouse. But no era shaped Berlin quite like the Cold War, a period where it became a microcosm of global tensions and a symbol of resilience in the face of division.

- **1945: Divided City, Divided World:** The scars of World War II ran deep, and Berlin was carved into four Allied sectors, with the Soviet zone becoming East Berlin and the remaining three forming West Berlin. This artificial division, a stark symbol of the ideological clash between capitalism and communism, set the stage for decades of drama.

- **1948-49: The Berlin Blockade and Airlift:** In a tense standoff, the Soviets choked off access to West Berlin, hoping to starve it into submission. But the Western Allies responded with the Berlin Airlift, a daring operation that kept the city alive with food and supplies for 11 months, a testament to unwavering resolve.

- **1961: The Wall Goes Up:** As East Germans fled in droves to the West, the Soviet-backed government built the infamous Berlin Wall, a concrete barrier, a chilling symbol of Cold War division. For 28 years, the Wall stood as a stark reminder of the human cost of ideological conflict.

- **1989: Fall of the Wall and Reunification:** In a wave of popular uprisings across Eastern Europe, the Berlin Wall finally crumbled in 1989, sparking jubilation and marking the end of an era. Germany reunified, and Berlin, once a divided city, symbolized hope and unity.

These are only a few pivotal moments that shaped Berlin's Cold War history. Each corner of the city holds stories of courage, defiance, and the unwavering human spirit. As you explore Berlin, remember these tales of the past, for they are ever-present in this remarkable city.

Berlin: A City Unbound by Borders

Berlin is a sprawling cityscape unlike any other. Instead of a neatly defined center, it meanders along the Spree River, embracing a mosaic of distinct districts, each with its spirited personality. Understanding its geography and layout unlocks the secrets of this chameleon-like city.

- **The City's Lifeline:** Flowing through the heart of Berlin, the Spree River isn't merely a natural landmark. It's the city's lifeblood. Bridges weave a connecting web, and its banks offer scenic strolls and prime people-watching.
- **Power and History:** At the city's center lies Mitte, a district where grand boulevards lined with majestic buildings shed light on Prussia's imperial past. Brandenburg Gate, Reichstag Building, and the poignant Holocaust Memorial are some historical treasures to be found here.
- **Edgy Charm and Counterculture:** Cross the Spree, and you'll find yourself in Kreuzberg-Friedrichshain, a haven for alternative culture. Street art explodes on colorful walls, trendy cafes buzz with creative energy, and nightlife thrums with a rebellious beat.
- **Family Haven and Trendy Hub:** For a taste of Berlin's family-friendly charm, head to Prenzlauer Berg. Cobbled streets lined with pastel-colored buildings and idyllic parks create a warm atmosphere, while hip cafes and independent shops add a touch of urban cool.
- **Elegance and Opulence:** Across the Tiergarten Park lies Charlottenburg-Wilmersdorf, a district exuding aristocratic grandeur. From the opulent Kurfürstendamm shopping boulevard to the sprawling Tiergarten Park, this area offers a glimpse into Berlin's lap of luxury.

This is only a brief snapshot of Berlin's diverse districts. Each neighborhood adds its brushstroke to the city's canvas, inviting you to discover its secrets and vibrant soul.

A Feast for the Senses: Berlin's Cultural Buffet

Berlin's heart isn't only etched in stone and history. It explodes in a rich symphony of art, music, and film, fueled by an insatiable creative spirit. This city is a canvas for artistic expression, a stage for musical experimentation, and a silver screen reflecting its turbulent past and hopeful future.

Berlin explodes in a rich symphony of art.

- **Art:** Beyond the iconic Spree River, the walls of galleries and abandoned spaces breathe life with street art bursting with color and social commentary. Renowned museums like the Alte Nationalgalerie and Bode Museum house treasures from antiquity, while cutting-edge contemporary art thrives in spaces like the KW Institute for Contemporary Art and Hamburger Bahnhof. Every corner beckons with artistic energy, urging you to lose yourself in its ever-evolving presence.

- **Music:** Berlin's pulse beats to the rhythm of a thousand drums. Classical notes echo in grand concert halls, while techno beats throb in underground clubs. Live music erupts from every corner, from smoky jazz bars to bustling beer gardens. Whether headbanging in Berghain or swaying to a symphony at the Philharmonie, Berlin's music scene guarantees an experience that goes straight to your soul.

- **Film:** Lights, camera, action. Berlin's cinematic legacy is woven into the fabric of the city. Historical landmarks like the Babylon cinema hold Marlene Dietrich's glamour, while independent theaters showcase cutting-edge arthouse films. The annual Berlinale festival draws cinephiles worldwide, transforming the city into a remarkable showcase of international cinema. So, grab your popcorn, settle in, and let Berlin's captivating stories unfold on the silver screen.

- **A Culinary Adventure:** Berlin's cultural feast is a delightful odyssey for your taste buds. Traditional delights like hearty currywurst and melt-in-your-mouth Pfannkuchen (Berlin's particular take on donuts) satisfy your cravings for comfort food. Michelin-starred restaurants push the boundaries of gastronomy, while delicious street food markets tempt you with flavors from around the world. Vegan cafes and organic delis cater to conscious palates, and trendy brunch spots fuel your exploration with delicious fuel. In Berlin, every bite is an adventure, every meal a cultural exchange.

From artistic explosions to musical mélanges and culinary journeys, this city keeps your senses perpetually entertained. Dive in, explore, and savor every drop of Berlin's vibrant cultural feast.

Berlin: A City Always in Motion

Berlin's calendar is a medley of lively events and festivals, ensuring there's always something to spark your interest, regardless of the season. Here's a taste of what awaits you throughout the year:

Winter:
- **Berlinale Film Festival:** February brings the glamour of the Berlin International Film Festival, showcasing the best of international cinema.
- **Long Night of Museums:** In late August, museums stay open late, offering educational experiences and special exhibits.
- **Christmas Markets:** Charming Christmas markets sprout across the city throughout December, tempting you with festive treats and handmade crafts.

Spring:
- **Maifest:** In May, beer gardens and parks come alive with the Maifest, a joyous celebration of spring with traditional music and food.
- **Karneval der Kulturen:** Join the vibrant Carnival of Cultures, celebrating Berlin's multicultural diversity with colorful costumes and infectious music.

Summer:

- **Fusion Festival:** For electronic music lovers, the Fusion Festival offers a lineup of DJs from far and wide and live acts set amid stunning natural surroundings.
- **Berlin Fashion Week:** The fashion world descends upon Berlin for Fashion Week, showcasing the latest trends and innovative designs.

Autumn:

- **Jazzfest Berlin:** Sail away on the strains of the jazz world with the Berlin Jazz Festival, featuring concerts by renowned and emerging artists.
- **Festival of Lights:** In autumn, usually between September and October, the city transforms into a magical wonderland with dazzling light installations adorning landmarks and streets.
- **Lollapalooza Berlin:** Get your groove on at Lollapalooza, a massive music festival featuring international headliners and up-and-coming artists.
- **Berlin Marathon:** Cheer on the runners at the Berlin Marathon, a prestigious event that winds through the city's iconic landmarks.

Sports in Berlin:

Berliners are a passionate bunch when it comes to sports. Here are popular activities and local teams to check out:

- **Football (Soccer):** Hertha BSC and FC Union Berlin is the city's top team, offering exciting matches and a raucous fan atmosphere.
- **Ice Hockey:** Eisbären Berlin is a dominant force in German ice hockey, with a loyal fanbase and electrifying games.
- **Basketball:** ALBA Berlin is a powerhouse in European basketball, attracting international talent and delivering high-octane action.
- **Cycling:** Berlin boasts a vast network of bike paths, making it a cyclist's paradise. Whether you are a casual rider or a cycling enthusiast, you'll find plenty of routes to explore.

Whether you crave cultural immersion, thrilling competition, or simply a vibrant atmosphere, Berlin has something to keep you entertained and engaged throughout the year. Lace up your shoes, grab your calendar, and get ready to experience the pulsating energy of this ever-evolving city.

Navigating Berlin: From U-Bahns to Bikes and Beyond

Thanks to its efficient and extensive public transportation system, getting around Berlin is a breeze. Whether you're a seasoned city hopper or a first-time visitor, navigating the city is easy and affordable.

Mastering the Transit Maze:

- **U-Bahn and S-Bahn:** The U-Bahn (underground) and S-Bahn (overground) are the backbone of Berlin's public transport. Buy a single ticket (Kurzstrecke) for short journeys or a Tageskarte (day ticket) for unlimited travel within zones. Download the BVG app for real-time schedules and route planning.
- **Buses and Trams:** Buses and trams complement the rail network, reaching smaller streets and neighborhoods. Validate your ticket upon boarding.
- **Bikes and Scooters:** Berlin is a cycling paradise with dedicated lanes and a bike-friendly culture. Rent a bike or scooter from numerous providers like Nextbike or Tier, explore at your pace, and join the two-wheeled revolution.

Travel Tips for a Smooth Ride:

- **Currency:** Euros are the German currency. ATMs and currency exchange offices are readily available. Consider using a travel debit card for better exchange rates.
- **Cultural Norms:** Berliners are generally friendly and helpful but consider cultural norms. Queue politely, avoid talking loudly on public transport, and don't expect everyone to speak English.
- **Seasonal Considerations:** Pack for all seasons. Summers are warm and sunny, while winters can be cold and snowy. Spring and autumn have pleasant temperatures and fewer crowds.

Bonus Tips:

- **Berlin Welcome Card:** Consider purchasing a Berlin Welcome Card for discounted travel, free entry to museums, and other perks.
- **Tipping:** Tipping is customary in restaurants or cafes, and rounding up your bill is appreciated.

- **Learn Some Basic German Phrases:** "Guten Tag" (hello), "Danke" (thank you), and "Bitte" (please). They go a long way.

Following these tips and embracing Berlin's spirit guarantees a smooth and unforgettable experience.

Berlin's Luminaries: A Galaxy of Historical and Contemporary Stars

Berlin's history and contemporary culture are rich with remarkable individuals who have left their mark on the city. From visionary thinkers to artistic trailblazers, here are the figures who shaped Berlin's iconic spirit:

History Makers:

- **Frederick the Great:** Prussia's iconic ruler, Frederick the Great, transformed Berlin from a sleepy town into a flourishing cultural and economic powerhouse. His architectural legacy, including the Brandenburg Gate and the Charlottenburg Palace, stands as a testament to his ambition.

- **Karl Marx and Friedrich Engels:** The intellectual fathers of communism, Karl Marx and Friedrich Engels, found refuge and inspiration in Berlin during their revolutionary activities. Their work continues to resonate globally, shaping political and economic thought.

- **Rosa Luxemburg:** A fiery socialist and feminist, Rosa Luxemburg challenged the status quo and fought for social justice in Berlin. Her unwavering commitment to workers' rights and her eloquent critiques of capitalism continue to inspire activists today.

- **Konrad Adenauer:** The first Chancellor of West Germany, Konrad Adenauer, played a pivotal role in rebuilding Berlin and West Germany after the devastation of World War II. His leadership during the Cold War helped shape the city's future as a democratic and prosperous nation.

- **Willy Brandt:** A champion of reconciliation and Ostpolitik, Willy Brandt's tenure as Chancellor of West Germany saw a thaw in relations with East Germany. His courageous decision to kneel at the Warsaw Ghetto memorial remains a powerful symbol of atonement and understanding.

Contemporary Icons:

- **David Bowie:** The enigmatic rock legend David Bowie found artistic refuge and inspiration in Cold War Berlin. His 1977 album "Heroes," recorded in the shadow of the Berlin Wall, became a powerful anthem of hope and defiance.

- **Marlene Dietrich:** The epitome of glamour and cinematic power, Marlene Dietrich's Berlin years solidified her status as a screen legend. Her performances in films like "The Blue Angel" and "M" captivated audiences and challenged gender norms.

- **Daniel Barenboim:** Renowned conductor and pianist Daniel Barenboim has called Berlin home for decades, leading the Staatskapelle Berlin orchestra and spearheading cultural initiatives like the Barenboim-Said Akademie. His commitment to music as a bridge between cultures has resonated deeply in the city.

- **Meret Oppenheim:** A surrealist artist whose work challenged societal expectations, Meret Oppenheim left an indelible mark on Berlin's artistic landscape. Her iconic "Object" (fur-lined teacup) continues to spark conversations about the nature of art and gender roles.

- **Wim Wenders:** One of German cinema's most celebrated directors, Wim Wenders' films have captured the essence of Berlin's divided past and hopeful present. His introspective and visually stunning works, like "Wings of Desire" and "Paris, Texas," offer diverse perspectives on the city's soul.

From political giants to artistic visionaries, these individuals have shaped the city's character and continue to inspire future generations. As you explore Berlin, keep these figures in mind, and their stories will add depth and meaning to your journey through this captivating city.

Local Customs, Traditions, and Celebrations

Berliners are a colorful mix of tradition and modern cool. Their customs and celebrations reflect this exciting blend. Go beyond the iconic sights and discover the cultural nuances that make Berlin tick to truly experience the city's soul.

Local Customs and Quirks:

- **Sunday Is Rest Day:** Sundays in Berlin are dedicated to relaxation and family time. Most shops are closed, giving a welcome respite from the urban rush. Embrace the leisurely pace and join the locals in parks, cafes, or bustling flea markets.
- **No "Hello" on Public Transport:** While Berliners are friendly, small talk on public transport isn't the norm. Keep a comfortable silence and avoid personal conversations. Headphones are your trusted companion.
- **Separating Trash Makes Sense:** Recycling is taken seriously in Berlin. Learn the sorting system (usually yellow for packaging, green for glass, blue for paper, and brown for bio-waste) and respect it diligently.
- **Queue Politely:** Patience is a virtue in Berlin. Form orderly lines at bakeries, museums, and public transport, and let everyone have their turn.

Participating with Respect:

- **Dress Modestly for Religious Sites:** When visiting churches, synagogues, or mosques, dress conservatively to show respect for local customs.
- **Avoid Loud Behavior:** Berliners value peace. Keep noise levels down in public spaces and respect residential areas' tranquility.
- **Learn Basic German:** Phrases like "Guten Tag" (hello), "Danke" (thank you), and "Bitte" (please) go a long way and show your appreciation for local culture.
- **Follow Event Etiquette:** Some festivals or celebrations may have specific protocols. Be mindful of signs and instructions and ask for a respectful and enjoyable experience if unsure.

By understanding these local customs, traditions, and celebrations, you will engage with Berlin on a deeper level. Embrace the quirks, participate respectfully in cultural events, and witness the soul of this dynamic city unfold before your eyes. Remember, cultural sensitivity unlocks the true magic of Berlin. Learn, observe, and enjoy the journey.

Unconventional Nightlife Thrills in Berlin

While Berlin's club scene hops with techno beats and electrifying vibes, the city's nocturnal adventures extend far beyond the dance floor. Here's a peek into the unconventional nightlife playground that awaits:

Immersive Experiences:

- **Silent Cinema:** Slip on headphones and lose yourself in a movie under the open sky at Kulturpark Friedrichshain's Freiluftkino. The shared silence and synchronized laughter create a memorable communal experience.
- **Speakeasy Soirees:** Uncover hidden bars tucked away behind unmarked doors and vintage bookcases. Indulge in secret cocktails, jazz melodies, and a touch of Prohibition-era mystery.
- **Virtual Voyages:** Dive into virtual reality worlds at VR arcades like Virtual Reality Lounge Berlin. Explore alien landscapes, battle monsters, or experience the thrill of skydiving – within the comfort of a dimly lit room.

Artistic Escapades:

- **Midnight Museum Mayhem:** Join the Long Night of Museums, an annual event where museums stay open late with pop-up performances, themed exhibits, and DJ sets, transforming historical halls into a playground of art and music.
- **Gallery Hopping:** Explore the remarkable Mitte art scene, with galleries offering a chance to rub shoulders with artists and fellow art enthusiasts.
- **Live Music Adventures:** Beyond the club scene, intimate jazz bars like Quasimodo and cozy concert halls like the Kesselhaus host soulful musical journeys across genres, from blues and folk to indie and experimental sounds.

Foodie Forays:

- **Street Food Safaris:** Embark on a late-night culinary adventure at Mauerpark Flea Market or Boxhagener Platz, where food trucks tempt your taste buds with global street delights, from Korean ramen to Venezuelan arepas.
- **Spätkauf Delights:** No matter the hour, Berlin's ubiquitous Spätkaufs have your back. These convenience stores offer everything from warm currywurst to late-night pastries, perfect for refueling after a night of exploration.
- **Rooftop Retreats:** Sip cocktails with panoramic city views at trendy rooftop bars. Take flight in the sparkling skyline and cool beats for a genuinely unforgettable Berlin night.

Travel Enhancements:

- **Berlin Welcome Card:** Invest in this travel pass for discounted public transport, free museum entry, and exclusive deals. Navigate the city seamlessly and maximize your cultural experience.

- **Bike Rentals:** Embrace Berlin's cycling culture and rent a bike to explore hidden corners, cruise along the Spree River, or join a guided tour for a sporting perspective.

- **Local Apps:** Download apps like BVG Fahrplan for finding your way around public transport, Airbnb for Berlin-style accommodations, and Mit Vergnügen for discovering nearby events and activities.

Remember: Be mindful of noise levels in residential areas, respect local customs, and dress appropriately for late-night adventures. With an open mind and adventurous spirit, Berlin's unconventional nightlife playground promises to ignite your senses and create unforgettable memories extending far beyond the traditional club scene.

As you venture deeper into Berlin's remarkable layers, you'll discover a city that defies definition. It's a haven for artists and creatives, a playground for foodies and nightlife enthusiasts, and a sanctuary for those seeking an escape from the ordinary. Whether you lose yourself in the hushed reverence of the Holocaust Memorial, marvel at the street art adorning the East Side Gallery, or dance the night away in a subterranean club, Berlin guarantees an experience that will stay etched in your memory long after you've left.

Chapter 2: To and From the Airport

Steel serpents thread their way through the clouds, disgorging travelers onto the gleaming expanse of Berlin Brandenburg Airport. Known affectionately as BER, it hums with the buzz of departure announcements and hurried footsteps, a gateway to adventure and homecoming. Opened after years of anticipation, BER stands as a testament to human ambition, rising from the ashes of delays and controversies to become the crown jewel of Berlin's air travel.

Map of Berlin's airports.
translation to en: skew-t (talk)derivative work: Hedavid (talk)Berlin.svg: Nodder, CC BY-SA 2.5 <https://creativecommons.org/licenses/by-sa/2.5>, via Wikimedia Commons. https://commons.wikimedia.org/wiki/File:Map_of_Berlin_airports.svg

Beyond the sleek façade and cutting-edge technology lies a heart that beats with the rhythm of human journeys, woven with tales of farewells, reunions, departures, and discoveries. In this chapter, you'll navigate the labyrinthine paths of BER, discovering the logistics and emotions that intertwine at this crossroads of destinations.

Arrival and Departure Navigation Made Easy

Berlin Brandenburg Airport might seem daunting at first glance. This streamlined section will equip you with the knowledge to navigate arrival and departure procedures, ensuring your Berlin adventure starts (and ends) smoothly.

Arriving at BER:

- **Touchdown:** Upon landing, follow the signs to baggage claim to collect your luggage. If you haven't checked in any bags, skip this step and head straight to passport control.

- **Passport Control:** Prepare your travel documents and answer questions with a smile. The queue length varies, so pack some patience or use the express lanes if available.

- **Customs:** Declare duty-free items you're bringing into Germany. Unsure? Follow the green "Nothing to Declare" lane or the red "Goods to Declare" lane, depending on your purchases.

- **Transportation Options:** Choose your next leg. Taxis line up outside the terminal or head to the train station within the airport for onward journeys. Public buses are available for budget-conscious travelers. Pre-booking an airport shuttle or ride-sharing service guarantees a smooth transition.

- **Information Desks:** Seek assistance if you're disoriented. Information desks are scattered throughout the terminal, ready to answer your questions and offer directions.

Departing from BER:

- **Check-in and Baggage Drop:** Head to your airline's designated check-in counters, present your travel documents, and check in your luggage. *Don't forget to weigh your bags beforehand to avoid excess baggage fees!*

- **Security Check:** Prepare for a security screening, ensuring your carry-on items comply with regulations. Liquids, electronics, and sharp objects must be placed in separate trays.

- **Passport Control:** Once again, show your passport and boarding pass. Take this opportunity to grab a coffee or browse the Duty-Free shops before settling at your gate.
- **Gate and Boarding:** Find your gate on the display boards and relax until boarding is announced. Be sure to listen for last-minute updates or gate changes.
- **Takeoff and Beyond:** Buckle up, enjoy the views, and prepare for your next adventure. Once airborne, you can unwind and let the friendly cabin crew guide you the rest of the way.

Transportation, Facilities, and Stress-Free Travel Tips

Berlin Brandenburg Airport (BER) bustles with arrivals and departures. With the correct information, finding your way will be a breeze. Here's a breakdown of transportation options, helpful facilities, and practical tips for a stress-free journey:

Transportation:

- **Trains:** The FEX and regional trains whisk you directly to Berlin Central Station and other city hotspots. S-Bahn trains connect to various city zones. Check timetables and platforms before boarding.
- **Buses:** Express buses like X7 and X71 offer direct connections to key areas. Budget-friendly buses connect to various suburbs. Purchase tickets at machines or using the BVG app (https://welcome2berlin.weebly.com/berlin-ticket-machine.html).
- **Taxis:** Lined up outside the terminals, taxis offer convenience but at a premium price. Consider ride-sharing apps like Uber for a more cost-effective option.
- **Car Rentals:** Several companies operate within the airport. Pre-booking can guarantee availability, especially during peak season.

Facilities and Services:

- **Information Desks:** Scattered throughout the terminals, friendly staff answer questions and give directions.
- **Lounges:** Airlines and independent operators offer paid access to comfortable spaces with refreshments and amenities like Wi-Fi and workstations.

- **Currency Exchange:** Several bureaus offer competitive exchange rates. ATMs are available for convenient cash withdrawals.
- **Food and Shops:** Many restaurants, cafes, and shops cater to a wide range of tastes and needs. Duty-free shopping awaits those departing from the EU.
- **Luggage Storage:** Store your bags for a fee if you have a layover or want to explore the city luggage-free.
- **Free Wi-Fi:** Stay connected throughout the airport with free Wi-Fi available in all terminal areas.

Practical Tips:

- **Download the BER Airport App:** Have real-time flight information, terminal maps, and transportation options at your fingertips!
- **Purchase a Berlin Welcome Card:** This discounted travel card provides unlimited rides on public transportation within Berlin and discounts on attractions.
- **Check Your Baggage Allowance:** Avoid excess baggage fees by weighing your bags beforehand. Pack light for short trips and use airport storage for more extended layovers.
- **Arrive Early for Departures:** Allow ample time for check-in, security checks, and boarding formalities. Download your boarding pass beforehand for a smoother process.
- **Plan Your Onward Journey:** Decide your transportation to your final destination in Berlin before you arrive. Make public transport connections or taxi bookings in advance if possible.
- **Relax and Enjoy:** Breathe, take in the atmosphere, and savor the excitement of your journey. BER is designed for your comfort and convenience.

Amenities, Services, and the Essentials

From the moment you touch down at Berlin Brandenburg Airport (BER), a medley of amenities and services will greet you, making your journey trouble-free and comfortable. Whether breezing through a layover or embarking on a grand adventure, BER offers everything you need to feel refreshed and prepared.

Inside the Terminal:

- **Foodie Paradise:** Indulge in a taste sensation culinary journey, from grab-and-go snacks to gourmet sit-down meals. Restaurants cater to all palates, from traditional German fare to international delights. Cafes offer aromatic coffee and baked treats, perfect for a quick pick-me-up.

- **Shopping Spree:** Explore a world of retail therapy with duty-free shops brimming with perfumes, cosmetics, and souvenirs. Designer boutiques and brand-name stores cater to fashionistas, while bookstores and convenience shops offer essentials and travel reads.

- **Relax and Recharge:** Need a moment of respite? Escape the hustle-bustle in one of the airport's quiet lounges. Enjoy complimentary Wi-Fi, comfortable seating, and refreshments while catching up on work or simply unwinding.

- **Stay Connected:** Don't lose touch. BER boasts free Wi-Fi throughout the terminals, allowing you to stay connected with loved ones or browse the web. Charge your devices at conveniently located charging stations and ensure you're always powered up.

- **Travel Essentials:** BER has you covered, from luggage storage to currency exchange. ATMs dispense local currency and currency exchange bureaus with competitive rates. Purchase a Berlin Welcome Card for discounted public transportation and access to attractions.

Beyond the Terminal:

- **Transportation Hub:** BER seamlessly connects you to the heart of Berlin and beyond. Trains whisk you directly to the city center, while buses and taxis offer another convenient way to get around. Car rental companies operate within the airport, making it easy to explore at your pace.

- **Accommodation Options:** Whether you have a long layover or need a crash pad before your flight, several hotels and guesthouses are located near the airport. Book in advance to secure your stay, especially during peak seasons.

- **City Exploration:** Don't let a layover go to waste. Explore the vibrant city of Schönefeld, which is nearby and known for its historical sites and charming cafes. Take a walk through the leafy Grunewald Forest (20 minutes from the airport) or visit the fascinating Technikmuseum Berlin (35 mintues from the airport).

Financial Matters:

- **Currency Exchange:** Several bureaus within the airport offer competitive rates for exchanging your currency. Compare rates before choosing a bureau to ensure you get the best deal.

- **ATMs:** Conveniently located ATMs dispense local currency, allowing you to withdraw cash without hassle. Remember to check your bank's fees for international withdrawals.

- **Luggage Services:** Need to store your bags for a layover or before your flight? BER offers secure luggage storage facilities for a fee. It frees you to explore the city without lugging your baggage around.

BER is a gateway to a world of possibilities. With its diverse amenities, convenient transportation options, and financial services, BER ensures your journey is as smooth and comfortable as possible.

Transportation Options for Every Traveler

Berlin Brandenburg Airport (BER) understands that one size doesn't fit all regarding travel preferences. Whether you're a budget-conscious backpacker, a time-pressed executive, or someone with accessibility needs, BER offers diverse transportation options to get you to your destination seamlessly.

For the Speedy Traveler:

- **Airport Express (FEX):** The fastest option, whisking you to Berlin Central Station in a sleek 30 minutes. Perfect for catching connecting flights or reaching the city center quickly.

- **S-Bahn Trains (S9 and S45):** Frequent services connect directly to various city zones, providing a convenient and affordable alternative to the FEX.

For the Budget-Conscious Explorer:

- **Express Buses (X7 and X71):** Direct connections to key areas, like Rudow and Alt-Mariendorf, are cost-effective options for those staying further out.

- **Regional Buses:** Connect to various suburbs and surrounding towns, ideal for budget-minded travelers venturing beyond the city center.

For the Eco-Friendly Adventurer:

- **Public Bicycles:** Rent a bike directly from the airport and cycle into the city, enjoying the fresh air and exercise. Bike lanes and dedicated infrastructure make getting around Berlin on two wheels a breeze.

- **Train and Walking:** Consider taking the train to a specific district and then walking to your final destination. Explore hidden alleyways and soak in the local atmosphere at a leisurely pace.

For Travelers with Mobility Needs:

- **Full Accessibility:** BER is fully accessible, with elevators, ramps, and wheelchair-accessible restrooms throughout the terminals.

- **Assistance Services:** Trained personnel are available to assist passengers with limited mobility, from baggage handling to boarding assistance.

- **Dedicated Vehicles:** Special buses and taxis equipped for wheelchairs ensure comfortable onward journeys.

Making an Informed Choice:

- **Information Desks:** Friendly staff at information desks will guide you on the best transportation option for your needs, budget, and destination.

- **BER Airport App:** Download the app for real-time schedules, platform information, and estimated travel times for available options.

- **Public Transport Tickets:** Purchase tickets at machines or through the BVG app before boarding buses or trams.

Planning your onward journey before arrival will save you time and stress. Research different options, factor in your budget and preferences, and choose the transportation mode that best suits your needs.

Option	Estimated Price (One Way)	Travel Time (to City Center)	Pros	Cons
FEX Airport Express Train	€4.40	30 minutes	Fastest, comfortable, direct to Central Station	Expensive
S-Bahn Train (S9 or S45)	€3.40	35-45 minutes	Affordable, frequent service, multiple stops	Slower than FEX, not as direct
Express Buses (X7 and X71)	€2.80	45-60 minutes	Budget-friendly, direct connections to specific areas	Slower than trains, limited destinations
Regional Buses	€2.80 - €4.80	45-60+ minutes	Affordable, reach further suburbs and towns	Slowest option, frequent transfers needed
Public Bicycles	€2/hour (initial)	45+ minutes (variable)	Eco-friendly, active travel, explore at your pace	Requires physical effort, weather dependent, limited availability

Train and Walking	€3.40 + Walking time	45+ minutes (variable)	Affordable, explore local area, customize your journey	Slower than direct options, requires walking
Airport Shuttle	€20-€40 (shared van)	30-45 minutes (variable)	Door-to-door service, convenient for groups	More expensive than public transport, limited scheduling flexibility
Taxi	€35-€50 (fixed fare)	25-35 minutes (variable)	Fastest, most convenient, door-to-door	Most expensive option, unpredictabl e traffic delays
Car Rental	€20-€50+ per day	20-30 minutes (variable)	Independen t travel, explore beyond the city center	Parking costs, rental fees, navigating unfamiliar roads

With a range of choices and readily available information, BER ensures every traveler can navigate the airport and onward journey easily, regardless of their budget, needs, or preferred pace.

Indulge in Luxury and Convenience

For those with discerning tastes and a willingness to splurge, Berlin Brandenburg Airport (BER) offers a buffet of premium services to pamper and expedite your journey. Step beyond the ordinary and embrace a touch of luxury:

Fast Forward Your Journey:

- **Private Transfers:** Skip the queues and traffic jams with a pre-booked limousine or luxury car. Arrive in style directly at your hotel or desired destination.
- **Fast Track Security:** Bypass the standard security lines and enjoy priority access, leaving you more time to relax or indulge in airport luxuries.

Unwind in Exquisite Comfort:

- **VIP Lounges:** Escape the hustle and bustle in exclusive airport lounges. Sink into plush seating, savor gourmet refreshments, and enjoy high-speed Wi-Fi, workspaces, and dedicated staff assistance.
- **Personal Shopping:** Don't settle for generic souvenirs. Arrange a personalized shopping experience and discover luxury brands and exclusive boutiques hidden within the airport terminals.

Indulge Your Culinary Side:

- **Restaurants:** Elevate your travel experience with exquisite culinary delights. Restaurants and gourmet eateries in the airport offer mouthwatering dishes and world-class service.
- **Private in-Flight Catering:** Pre-order gourmet meals and premium beverages for your flight, transforming your journey into a luxurious, personal dining experience.
- **Champagne Bars:** Celebrate your arrival or toast to a successful trip with a glass of bubbly at a stylish airport champagne bar.

Remember:

- Book premium services in advance, especially during peak seasons, to guarantee availability.
- Research various providers and compare prices to find the perfect fit for your budget.
- Consider combining services for a seamless and luxurious travel experience from arrival to departure.

BER settles into a quiet rhythm as the last wheels leave the tarmac, painting a fiery streak across the twilight sky. Departure gates stand sentinel, awaiting the dawn of new departures, while weary travelers slump gratefully into waiting taxis, eager to embrace the city. Though its walls bear the tales of a thousand destinations, BER remains tethered to Berlin, a constant pulse in the city's ever-expanding heart. In the closing sounds of departing engines, the promise of new beginnings lingers, reminding you that regardless of how far you stray, the journey always starts and ends somewhere called *home.*

Chapter 3: Mitte – Charlottenburg-Wilmersdorf

Mitte and Charlottenburg-Wilmersdorf, nestled within the heart of Berlin, beckon travelers with a captivating history and contemporary allure. As you traverse cobbled streets, grand avenues, and sprawling parks, prepare to be swept away by a whirlwind of iconic landmarks, vibrant art scenes, and a palpable hum of energy.

Mitte, Berlin.

In Mitte, the city's beating heart, iconic monuments like the Brandenburg Gate and the Reichstag silently witness a turbulent past. Trendy cafes and avant-garde galleries dance with the rhythm of a vibrant presence. Across the Spree River, Charlottenburg-Wilmersdorf offers a contrasting quiet charm, with the aristocratic elegance of Charlottenburg Palace and the lush expanse of Tiergarten Park providing a welcome respite from the urban buzz.

Mitte: Where Berlin's Past Mingles with the Present

Mitte, meaning "Center," is the beating heart of Berlin. From its majestic monuments to its art galleries buzzing with contemporary energy, Mitte encapsulates the very essence of this captivating city.

Historical Background

Mitte's story speaks of the rise and fall of empires. Originally a small trading settlement on the Spree River, it blossomed as the heart of Berlin, housing Prussian royalty and witnessing the city's cultural golden age. In the tumult of the 20th century, it became a divided wasteland during the Cold War, only to reemerge as a unified and lively district after the fall of the Wall. Today, Mitte wears its history on its sleeve, blending iconic landmarks with a modern touch, inviting visitors to discover its layers of stories.

Main Attractions

Mitte's rich collection of attractions draws visitors from all corners of the globe. Here are a few must-sees:

- **Brandenburg Gate:** A symbol of unity and resilience, this neoclassical monument offers stunning views and a palpable historical aura.

The Brandenburg Gate.

- **Museum Island:** Astound yourself with world-class art and antiquities at museums like the Pergamon Museum, Bode Museum, and Neues Museum.

  Of course, every museum has its own hours. Still, generally, as of the writing of this book, the regular opening hours are from 10 am – 5 or 6 pm from Tuesday to Sunday (Altes Museum and Bode Museum are closed on Tuesday), but please always double-check the opening hours online should there have been any slight changes in their schedule.

Museum Island.

- **Reichstag Building:** Witness the seat of German democracy and climb the iconic glass dome for breathtaking city panoramas.

  As of the writing of this book, the regular opening hours are from 8 am to midnight, 7 days a week, but please always double-check the opening hours online should there have been any slight changes in their schedule.

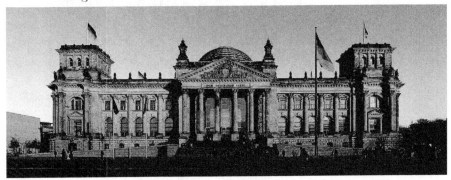

Reichstag Building.

- **Holocaust Memorial:** Reflect on the sad reality of the past in this moving field of concrete slabs, a poignant reminder of Holocaust victims.

Holocaust Memorial.

- **Gendarmenmarkt:** This picturesque square is perfect for strolling and soaking in the cultural spirit with its majestic cathedrals and lively atmosphere.

Gendarmenmarkt.

- **Berlin Wall Memorial:** Walk along the preserved section of the Wall and explore the Documentation Center to delve deeper into this pivotal period in Berlin's history.

Berlin Wall Memorial.

- **Hackesche Höfe:** Wander through this charming complex of courtyards dotted with art galleries, cafes, and curious shops.

Hackesche Höfe.

Avil111 dr. Avishai Teicher, CC BY-SA 4.0 <https://creativecommons.org/licenses/by-sa/4.0>, via Wikimedia Commons.
https://commons.wikimedia.org/wiki/File:Hackesche_H%C3%B6fe_No_1.jpg

- **Berlin Palace:** Explore the reconstructed Berliner Stadtschloss, now housing the Humboldt Forum, a cultural hub dedicated to world history and art.

As of the writing of this book, the regular opening hours are from 10 am to 8 pm from Wednesday to Monday, but please always double-check the opening hours online should there have been any slight changes in their schedule.

Berlin Palace.
https://www.pexels.com/photo/building-with-dome-roof-10674689/

Transport

Getting around Mitte is a breeze using its comprehensive transportation network.

- **U-Bahn and S-Bahn:** The city's efficient underground and regional train system provides easy access to all corners of the district and beyond.
- **Trams:** Hop on a nostalgic tram for a scenic ride through Mitte's historic streets.
- **Buses:** Buses provide another convenient option for local travel.
- **Bikes:** Rent a bike and explore at your own pace, navigating the well-developed cycle paths throughout the area.
- **Walking:** Mitte is best explored on foot so that you can savor the architectural details and vibrant atmosphere.

Did You Know: The Brandenburg Gate, once marking the border between East and West Berlin, was the location of President Reagan's famous "Tear down this wall" speech in 1987.

Experiences

Beyond the iconic sights, Mitte offers a wealth of experiences:

- **Thematic Tours:** Explore the district through themed walking tours, like "Third Reich Berlin" or "Street Art Tour," to better understand its diverse history and contemporary culture.
- **Festivals and Events:** From Christmas markets and open-air cinema screenings to art exhibitions and street festivals, Mitte's calendar is brimming with vibrant events throughout the year.
- **Museum Nights:** Experience museums after dark with extended hours, special exhibits, and live music, creating an intriguing, atmospheric way to explore art and history.
- **Boat Tours:** Glide along the Spree River for a water-borne perspective of Mitte's landmarks and discover hidden gems along the waterfront.

Family Fun

Traveling with little ones? Mitte has plenty to keep them entertained:

- **Zoologischer Garten Berlin:** Discover a fascinating world of animals at one of the oldest zoos in Germany.
- **Aquarium Berlin:** Dive into the underwater world and marvel at the colorful fish and marine life.
- **Spreeuferpark:** Enjoy a picnic or play games in this sprawling park, with scenic river views and ample green space for families to unwind.
- **Museum für Kommunikation:** Step into a world of communication, from ancient printing presses to the latest virtual reality technology. Interactive exhibits make learning about communication history engaging and educational.

Did You Know: The iconic Unter den Linden boulevard running through Mitte was once lined with lime trees planted by Frederick the Great in the 17th century.

Where to Eat

Every foodie will be delighted by the culinary scene in Mitte, with a cornucopia of options to satisfy every taste bud.

- **Michelin-Starred Restaurants:** Indulge in exquisite fine dining at renowned restaurants like Rutz and Facil.
- **International Cuisine:** Embark on a global culinary journey with eateries representing flavors from Asia to Italy, Mexico to Argentina.
- **Traditional German Fare:** Savor hearty local specialties like schnitzel and currywurst at gemütliche biergartens or cozy pubs.
- **Street Food and Cafes:** Grab a quick bite at bustling currywurst stands, trendy food trucks, or charming cafes serving coffee and sweet treats.
- **Markets:** Explore vibrant farmers' markets overflowing with fresh produce and artisanal goods, or savor delicious street food at Markthalle IX.

Shopping Guide

Mitte's shopping scene caters to every style and budget, from art galleries showcasing contemporary creations to boutiques packed with vintage treasures.

- **Luxury Brands:** Explore flagship stores of renowned fashion houses like Louis Vuitton and Hugo Boss along the Friedrichstrasse.
- **Independent Boutiques:** Discover beautiful designs, handcrafted jewelry, and homeware in charming local shops tucked away in narrow alleys.
- **Art Galleries:** Browse stunning artwork and photography from emerging and established artists at galleries along Auguststrasse and Linienstrasse.
- **Hackescher Markt:** Wander through this labyrinthine complex of courtyards, home to a diverse selection of shops, from quirky souvenir stores to designer clothing boutiques.
- **Flohmarkt am Mauerpark:** Hunt for vintage treasures and one-of-a-kind finds at this popular flea market held every Sunday along the Berlin Wall.

Did You Know: The Museum Island (Museumsinsel) was previously known as Spreeinsel (Spree Island) and was the city center in the Middle Ages.

Entertainment

After a day of sightseeing and exploring, explore Mitte's lively nightlife scene:

- **Theater and Opera:** Catch a breathtaking performance at renowned venues like the Komische Oper Berlin or Deutsches Theater.
- **Live Music:** Enjoy live music at intimate jazz bars, pulsating nightclubs, or open-air concerts in the summer months.
- **Cinemas:** See the latest blockbusters or independent films at historic cinemas like Babylon or Kino Babylon Mitte.
- **Rooftop Bars:** Sip cocktails and soak in breathtaking city views from trendy rooftop bars like Rooftop One Bar.
- **Late-Night Cafes:** Fuel your creative energy or chat with friends at cozy cafes open until the early hours.

Did You Know: The Hackesche Höfe courtyard complex was a gathering place for artists and bohemians in the early 20th century and played a significant role in Berlin's cultural scene.

Sports and Leisure

Stay active and unwind with these recreational options in Mitte:

- **Tiergarten:** Escape the urban buzz and enjoy a stroll or bike ride through this sprawling park, a green oasis in the heart of the city.
- **Spree River Cruises:** Enjoy a relaxing cruise along the Spree River and admire the city's landmarks from a watery perspective.
- **Yoga and Pilates:** Find your inner zen at numerous studios offering yoga, Pilates, and other fitness classes.
- **Swimming Pools:** Beat the heat or exercise at indoor or outdoor pools, like Stadtbad Mitte.
- **Boat and Bike Rentals:** Rent a boat or bike and explore the city's waterways and cycle paths at your own pace.

Accommodations

Mitte has a range of accommodation options for every budget and traveler type:

- **Luxury Hotels:** Experience five-star service and opulence at hotels like The Ritz-Carlton or Hotel Adlon Kempinski.

- **Boutique Hotels:** Find stylish and intimate stays with warm, inviting ambiance at smaller hotels, like Hotel Château Royal or Garden Living Berlin.
- **Apartments and Vacation Rentals:** Enjoy the comfort and privacy of a fully equipped apartment or rental in charming neighborhoods like Prenzlauer Berg or Mitte's historical center.
- **Hostels and Budget-Friendly Options:** Backpackers and budget travelers can find affordable dorms and private rooms at hostels like Generator Berlin Mitte or The Circus Hostel.

Whether you're drawn to its historical grandeur, bustling cultural scene, or trendy vibes, Mitte promises an unforgettable experience. Come and discover the essence of Berlin in this dynamic and multifaceted district, where the past harmoniously blends with the present's rhythm.

Charlottenburg-Wilmersdorf: Where Berlin's Opulence Meets Greenery

Charlottenburg-Wilmersdorf is a district seamlessly blending regal history with modern vibrancy. From sprawling forests to opulent palaces, it offers experiences for every traveler. It's time to explore this corner of the German capital, where grandeur and nature paint a picture-postcard of Berliner charm.

Historical Background

Charlottenburg's journey began in the 17th century with the construction of Schloss Charlottenburg. This majestic baroque palace, commissioned by Sophie Charlotte, Queen of Prussia, laid the foundation for what would become a bustling city center. In the 19th century, Kurfürstendamm emerged as a fashionable boulevard, attracting the cream of high society and transforming the area into Berlin's "West End." Through turbulent times, including the devastation of WWII and the Cold War division, Charlottenburg-Wilmersdorf has persevered, emerging with a fascinating blend of old and new grandeur and grit.

Main Attractions

- **Schloss Charlottenburg:** Immerse yourself in Prussian opulence through the palace's lavish chambers, gilded interiors, and sprawling gardens. Admire the delicate porcelain collection in the Porcelain Cabinet and marvel at the grandeur of the New Wing.

  As of the writing of this book, the regular opening hours are from 10 am to 5:30 pm from Tuesday to Sunday (closed on Monday), but please always double-check the opening hours online should there have been any slight changes in their schedule.

Schloss Charlottenburg.
acediscovery, CC BY 4.0 <https://creativecommons.org/licenses/by/4.0>, via Wikimedia Commons
https://commons.wikimedia.org/wiki/File:Schloss-Charlottenburg_Berlin.jpg

- **Kurfürstendamm (Ku'damm):** Stroll along this iconic avenue, a paradise for shoppers seeking luxury brands and trendy boutiques. Catch a sizzling theater show, marvel at street performers, or indulge in a gourmet meal at an upscale restaurant.

You can visit any time you want. Shops are usually open by 9 am.

Kurfürstendamm.
Maksym Kozlenko, CC BY-SA 4.0 <https://creativecommons.org/licenses/by-sa/4.0>, via Wikimedia Commons. https://commons.wikimedia.org/wiki/File:2023-01-23_Kurf%C3%BCrstendamm_(Berlin-Charlottenburg)_3.jpg

- **Kaiser Wilhelm Memorial Church:** Stand amid the ruins, a sobering reminder of WWII's destruction. Climb the tower for panoramic city views and learn about the church's fascinating history and reconstruction efforts in the adjacent exhibition.

As of the writing of this book, the regular opening hours are from 10 am to 6 pm every day, but please always double-check the opening hours online should there have been any slight changes in their schedule.

Kaiser Wilhelm Memorial Church.
https://www.pexels.com/photo/kaiser-wilhelm-memorial-church-in-berlin-12042140/

- **Teufelsberg:** Hike up this former Cold War listening station for panoramic views and a glimpse into espionage history. British and American intelligence used the former Cold War listening station to spy on East Germany. Explore the abandoned buildings, learn about the site's transformation into an art space, and witness stunning Berlin sunsets.

As of the writing of this book, the regular opening hours are from 11 am to sunset every day, but please always double-check the opening hours online should there have been any slight changes in their schedule.

Teufelsberg.
https://www.pexels.com/photo/building-on-the-teufelsberg-peak-in-berlin-germany-14454351/

- **Lietzensee Park:** Seek tranquility by this picturesque lake. Rent a boat, sunbathe on the grassy shores, or stroll along the winding paths surrounded by lush greenery.

  You can visit any time you want.

Lietzensee Park.
Fridolin freudenfett (Peter Kuley), CC BY-SA 3.0 <https://creativecommons.org/licenses/by-sa/3.0>, via Wikimedia Commons.
https://commons.wikimedia.org/wiki/File:Charlottenburg_LietzenseePark-4.jpg

- **The Olympic Stadium:** Feel the electrifying energy of a sporting event or concert within this historic stadium. To discover its fascinating past, take a tour and witness the torch that once blazed during the 1936 Olympics.

As of the writing of this book, the normal opening hours are from 10 am to 7 pm every day except on event days. However, please always double-check the opening hours online should there have been any slight changes in their schedule.

The Olympic Stadium.
https://www.pexels.com/photo/stadium-in-sunlight-19088063/

- **Grunewald Forest and Tower:** Escape the urban jungle and lose yourself in the vast expanse of the Grunewald Forest. Hike or cycle through the shady trails, spot diverse wildlife, and ascend the Grunewald Tower for breathtaking city panoramas.

As of the writing of this book, the normal opening hours for the tower are from 10 am to 10 pm from Monday to Sunday, but please always double-check the opening hours online should there have been any slight changes in their schedule. You can visit the forest itself at any time.

Grunewald Tower.
Leonhard Lenz, CC0, via Wikimedia Commons.
https://commons.wikimedia.org/wiki/File:Grunewaldturm_2020-07-12_02.jpg

Transport

- **U-Bahn and S-Bahn:** Charlottenburg-Wilmersdorf is well-connected by Berlin's extensive public transportation network. U-Bahn lines U7 and U1 and S-Bahn lines S9, S7 and S5 provide convenient access to all major attractions.
- **Buses and Trams:** Numerous bus and tram lines crisscross the district, providing additional transportation options and a chance to experience the city from a street-level perspective.
- **Bicycles:** Rent a bike and explore the area at your own pace, making the most of Charlottenburg-Wilmersdorf's cycle-friendly paths and avenues.

Experiences

- **Theatrical Delights:** From classic operas at the Deutsche Oper Berlin to avant-garde performances at the Schaubühne am Lehniner Platz, Charlottenburg-Wilmersdorf caters to all theatrical tastes.
- **Foodie Adventures:** Embark on a culinary journey through diverse cuisines, from Michelin-starred restaurants like Prism to quirky cafes and authentic Turkish eateries.
- **Historical Insights:** Join walking tours of Kurfürstendamm, discover Cold War history at Teufelsberg, or enjoy a boat tour on Lietzensee to find the district's hidden gems.

Family Fun

- **Zoo Berlin:** Discover fascinating animals from around the world at one of Europe's oldest and largest zoos.
- **Spielplatz im Grunewald:** Let your little ones loose in this sprawling forest playground. Swings, slides, climbing frames, and sandpits guarantee hours of fun while parents can relax under the shade of towering trees.
- **Grunewaldsee:** Explore the tranquil waters of this lake, surrounded by lush greenery, and take a dip. Pack a picnic basket and enjoy a family feast by the water's edge.

Where to Eat

- **Dicke Wirtin:** Savor hearty German fare in this traditional pub frequented by locals and celebrities. The roast pork knuckle and apple strudel are must-tries.

- **Marjellchen:** Indulge in modern European cuisine, focusing on fresh, seasonal ingredients. The stylish yet relaxed atmosphere makes it perfect for a special occasion.
- **Kantini:** For a quick and healthy bite, Kantini offers delicious salads, sandwiches, and soups made with fresh, local ingredients.

Shopping Guide

- **Breitscheidplatz:** Discover high-end fashion brands like Gucci, Prada, and others on this elegant square adjacent to Kurfürstendamm.
- **Wilmersdorfer Straße:** Find trendy boutiques and local designer stores offering clothing, accessories, and homeware.
- **Karstadt:** Enjoy a shopping heaven at this department store, housing everything from luxury brands to everyday essentials.
- **Bikini Berlin:** Housed in a former parking garage, this concept mall is a haven for hipsters and fashionistas, with independent boutiques, trendy cafes, and art installations.

Did You Know: Once a Nazi propaganda tool, the Olympic Stadium hosted the legendary 1972 Summer Olympics, symbolizing post-war reconciliation.

Entertainment

- **Theater des Westens:** Catch a musical, operetta, or contemporary play at this historic theater on Ku'damm.
- **Schaubühne am Lehniner Platz:** Witness groundbreaking and experimental performances at this renowned theater known for its avant-garde productions.
- **Delphi Filmpalast:** Enjoy the latest blockbusters or independent films at one of these modern cinemas, offering comfortable seating and state-of-the-art technology.
- **Bikini Berlin:** Browse contemporary art exhibitions, shop at trendy stores, and enjoy panoramic city views from the rooftop terrace of this unusual cultural space housed in former industrial buildings.

Sports and Leisure

- **Grunewald Forest:** Hike or bike through the trails, rent a boat on the Grunewaldsee, or horseback riding at the Gutspark Pferdehof.

- **Olympiastadion:** Attend a football match or other sporting events, take a stadium tour, or go ice skating on the rink during winter.
- **Sport and Spaß Wilmersdorf:** Get active at this leisure center, which has swimming pools, fitness classes, saunas, and outdoor sports facilities.
- **Tennis Borussia Berlin:** Cheer on the local football team, Tennis Borussia Berlin, at their stadium in Charlottenburg.

Did You Know: Grunewald Forest is home to Europe's oldest oak tree, the "Dicke Eiche," estimated to be around 800 years old.

Accommodations

- **Hotel am Steinplatz:** Luxuriate in the elegance of this stunning hotel, featuring spacious rooms, a spa, and a rooftop terrace with spectacular city views.
- **Hotel Zoo:** Experience modern design and urban vibes at this stylish hotel close to the Kurfürstendamm.
- **Pension Peters:** Find budget-friendly accommodation with a charming atmosphere at this family-run guesthouse.
- **Hotel Savoy:** Enjoy a relaxed stay with personalized service at this traditional hotel in the heart of Wilmersdorf.
- **Airbnb:** For a genuinely local experience, rent an apartment or room through Airbnb and get insider tips from your hosts.

Did You Know: The district boasts several museums, each offering a glimpse into Berlin's rich history and culture.

As the sun dips below the horizon, casting long shadows across the cityscape, the charm of Mitte and Charlottenburg-Wilmersdorf takes on a new dimension. Gaslight lamps illuminate hidden alleys, while laughter spills from bustling biergartens, and the clinking of glasses echoes from rooftop bars.

Whether you're drawn to the pulsating energy of Mitte's nightlife or the serene beauty of Charlottenburg's palaces and gardens, these districts offer a kaleidoscope of experiences guaranteed to leave you with a lasting impression of Berlin's captivating spirit.

Chapter 4: Kreuzberg-Friedrichshain – Lichtenberg

Emerging from the shadows of the Cold War, Kreuzberg-Friedrichshain throbs with a potent blend of history, art, and urban grit. Once divided by the Berlin Wall, these multi-storied districts now stand united, their streets alive with cultural experiences. Stepping away from the central hubbub, Lichtenberg presents a tranquil haven within the bustling metropolis. Lush green spaces like Tierpark Berlin and Rummelsburger Bucht offer green leafy retreats. Prepare to be captivated by these districts' electrifying spirits, where the past harmonizes with the audacious beat of the present.

Kreuzberg-Friedrichshain

Welcome to Kreuzberg-Friedrichshain, a kaleidoscope of Berlin where gritty streetscapes paint urban canvases, history murmurs from weathered walls, and the pulse of music throbs through art-lined avenues. Once divided by the Berlin Wall, these districts are now perfect examples of multicultural harmony, energetic nightlife, and hidden green oases. Get ready to dive into the heart of Berlin's alternative scene, where every corner promises a story, and every beat invites you to move.

Main Attractions

Kreuzberg-Friedrichshain is a feast for the senses, bursting with sights, sounds, and flavors. Here are a few must-sees:

- **Görlitzer Park:** Soak up the multicultural sun in this vibrant park, where picnic blankets spread beside lively murals and community events buzz with life.

You can visit any time you want.

Görlitzer Park.

Chris Alban Hansen, CC BY-SA 2.0 <https://creativecommons.org/licenses/by-sa/2.0>, via Wikimedia Commons.
https://commons.wikimedia.org/wiki/File:G%C3%B6rlitzer_Park,_Berlin.jpg

- **Viktoriapark:** Escape the urban jungle to this serene oasis, where a cascading waterfall offers a peaceful soundtrack and panoramic views from the hilltop.

  You can visit any time you want.

Viktoriapark.

Neuköllner, CC BY-SA 4.0 <https://creativecommons.org/licenses/by-sa/4.0>, via Wikimedia Commons.
https://commons.wikimedia.org/wiki/File:%22Der_seltene_Fang%22_von_Ernst_Herter_(1896),_Viktoriapark,_Berlin-Kreuzberg.jpg

- **Markthalle Neun:** Sample culinary delights from around the world in this bustling market hall. It's a foodie haven with fresh produce, street vendors, and gourmet events.

As of the writing of this book, the normal opening hours are from 12 pm to 6 pm from Monday to Wednesday, 12 pm to 10 pm on Thursday, and 10 am to 6 pm on Saturday, but please always double-check the opening hours online should there have been any slight changes in their schedule.

Markthalle Neun.
https://www.pexels.com/photo/unks-coffee-shop-4543109/

- **Jewish Museum Berlin:** Journey through Jewish history and culture, confronting painful chapters and celebrating their remarkable resilience in this comprehensive museum.

As of the writing of this book, the normal opening hours are from 10 am to 6 pm from Monday to Sunday, but please always double-check the opening hours online should there have been any slight changes in their schedule.

Jewish Museum Berlin.

- **Deutsches Technikmuseum:** Ignite your inner inventor at this vast museum, a playground of locomotives, vintage planes, and interactive exhibits showcasing technological feats through the ages.

As of the writing of this book, the normal opening hours are from 9 am to 5:30 pm from Tuesday to Friday and from 10 am to 6 pm from Saturday to Sunday, but please always double-check the opening hours online should there have been any slight changes in their schedule.

Deutsches Technikmuseum.

- **Wall Museum-Checkpoint Charlie:** Stand where history walked, at the iconic Cold War border crossing. Replica barriers and exhibits paint a vivid picture of a divided city.

As of the writing of this book, the normal opening hours are from 10 am to 8 pm from Monday to Sunday, but please always double-check the opening hours online should there have been any slight changes in their schedule.

Wall Museum-Checkpoint Charlie.
Jörg Zägel, CC BY-SA 3.0 <https://creativecommons.org/licenses/by-sa/3.0>, via Wikimedia Commons. https://commons.wikimedia.org/wiki/File:Berlin,_Kreuzberg,_Friedrichstrasse_43-44,_Haus_am_Checkpoint_Charlie.jpg

- **Topography of Terror:** Witness the chilling reality of Nazi rule on the very grounds where the Gestapo and SS once operated. This sobering museum is a vital reminder of the importance of freedom and vigilance.

As of the writing of this book, the normal opening hours are from 10 am to 8 pm from Monday to Sunday, but please always double-check the opening hours online should there have been any slight changes in their schedule.

Topography of Terror.

- **East Side Gallery:** Witness the longest remaining stretch of the Berlin Wall transformed into an open-air art gallery, where murals speak of unity and freedom.

You can visit any time you want.

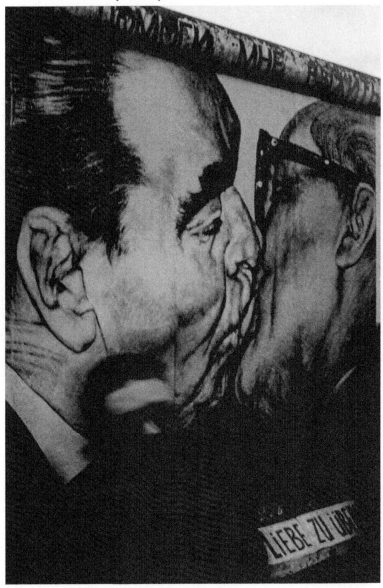

East Side Gallery.

- **RAW-Gelände:** Immerse yourself in the raw energy of this creative hub, where industrial spaces host underground bars, street art displays, and a vibrant independent spirit.

You can visit any time you want.

RAW-Gelände.

- **Boxhagener Platz:** Wander through this charming square, a magnet for locals and tourists. Browse the flea market's treasures, sip coffee at a sidewalk cafe, and soak up the buzzing atmosphere.

As of the writing of this book, the normal opening hours are from 10 am to 8 pm from Monday to Sunday, but please always double-check the opening hours online should there have been any slight changes in their schedule.

Boxhagener Platz.

Did You Know: Before its bohemian reincarnation, Kreuzberg was a working-class immigrant haven, harboring Turkish communities and punk squats.

Transport

Navigating this dynamic district is a breeze with numerous options:

- **U-Bahn (Underground Train):** The U1, U3, and U8 lines crisscross the area, making it easy to reach major attractions.
- **S-Bahn (City Train):** Lines S1, S5, S7, S9 and S25 stop at prominent landmarks like Ostkreuz and Warschauer Straße.
- **Bicycles:** Rent a bike and explore at your own pace, following dedicated bike lanes and discovering hidden corners.
- **Walking:** Lace up your shoes and get lost in the maze of streets, stumbling upon unexpected delights and immersing yourself in the local vibe.

Experiences

Dive deeper into the heart of Kreuzberg-Friedrichshain with these excursions:

- **Street Art Tours:** Paint the town (figuratively) with expert guides, uncovering hidden murals, learning about local artists, and deciphering the messages hidden in their urban canvas.
- **Alternative Berlin Tours:** Venture beyond the mainstream with off-the-beaten-path tours exploring historical squats, punk havens, and hidden gems whispered about only in local circles.
- **Live Music Nights:** Let the rhythm guide you through Friedrichshain's legendary nightlife scene, hopping between eclectic live music venues and underground clubs pulsating with diverse musical genres.
- **Spree River Boat Tours:** Float effortlessly through the heart of the district, admiring iconic landmarks like the Oberbaumbrücke and East Side Gallery, accompanied by historical storytelling and local tips.
- **Culinary Adventures:** Embark on a food tour through Kreuzberg's labyrinthine streets, sampling culinary delights from Turkish döner kebabs to Korean street food, Ethiopian stews to Vietnamese pho.
- **Community Events:** Surprise yourself with the multicultural offerings of the district by joining local festivals, street markets, artist's open studios, and neighborhood gatherings. It's a great way to connect with residents and experience the area's true spirit.

Did You Know: Friedrichshain's notorious Berghain techno club housed a power plant until the 1980s, explaining its industrial-chic aesthetic.

Did You Know: The Oberbaumbrücke Bridge once formed the border between East and West Berlin, and the iconic towers were border control checkpoints.

Where to Eat

This culinary melting pot caters to every craving, from budget-friendly bites to gourmet feasts:

- **Currywurst:** Sample Berlin's iconic currywurst sausage, with its spicy kick and myriad toppings, at Curry 36.
- **Falafel:** Dive into the vibrant flavors of the Middle East at Marooush, known for its fluffy falafel pitas and delicious hummus.
- **Vietnamese Street Food:** Experience the bustling atmosphere of Miss Saigon Restaurant, savoring authentic phởnoodle soup and fresh spring rolls.
- **Fine Dining:** Treat your taste buds to a gourmet adventure at Nobelhart & Schmutzig, serving innovative dishes in a quirky, industrial setting.
- **Craft Beer:** Quench your thirst at BRLO, Berlin's largest craft brewery, offering a range of innovative brews served in a lively atmosphere.
- **German Beer Garden Experience:** Raise a glass and soak up the lively atmosphere at a traditional beer garden, like Golgatha Biergarten, where laughter mingles with the clinking of steins.

Did You Know: East Side Gallery's "Kiss of Death" mural was painted by Dmitri Vrubel, inspired by Leonid Brezhnev's embrace with East German leader Erich Honecker.

Shopping Guide

From vintage treasures to high-end fashion, this shopper's paradise caters to all styles:

- **Boxhagener Platz Flea Market:** Hunt for vintage finds, handmade crafts, and local art at this sprawling weekend market.
- **Simon-Dach-Straße:** Explore this trendy street lined with independent chic boutiques, concept stores, and vintage shops.

- **RAW-Gelände:** Discover up-and-coming Berlin designers and streetwear labels at this creative hub's independent shops and pop-up markets.
- **Second-Hand Stores:** Unearth hidden gems at charming second-hand shops like Humana Vintage and Kleiderkammer, offering sustainable fashion finds at affordable prices.

Entertainment

With its vibrant nightlife and cultural energy, Kreuzberg-Friedrichshain offers a smorgasbord of entertainment:

- **Berghain:** Experience this world-renowned club's legendary techno beats and pulsating energy – a pilgrimage for clubbers and music lovers worldwide.
- **Yorck-Kino:** Catch independent films and international classics at this cozy cinema, with a charming atmosphere and curated programs.
- **Open-Air Cinemas:** Enjoy film screenings under the stars during the summer months at Freiluftkino Friedrichshain, featuring a mix of popular blockbusters and indie gems.

Did You Know: Boxhagener Platz flea market is one of the city's largest markets, with over 200 vendors offering vintage treasures, handcrafted goods, and street food.

Sports and Leisure

Get your adrenaline pumping or find serene relaxation in this dynamic district:

- **Water Sports:** Kayak or paddleboard down the Spree River, getting a water-eye-level perspective of the city and a refreshing workout.
- **Skate Parks:** Shred the ramps and grind the rails at Skatehalle Berlin or Park am Gleisdreieck, which are popular hangouts for the skating community.
- **Hiking and Biking:** Explore the green havens of Viktoriapark, which offers tranquil trails and panoramic views and is perfect for a scenic walk or bike ride.
- **Yoga and Fitness:** Unwind and recharge at studios like Yoga Verde or Yaam Berlin, offering diverse yoga classes, meditation sessions, and fitness centers.

- **Green Markets:** Browse for fresh produce, flowers, and handcrafted goods at the remarkable Arkonaplatz or Kollwitzplatz markets, soaking up the local atmosphere.

Accommodations

Find your perfect home away from home in this diverse district:

- **Boutique Hotels:** Experience stylish design and personalized service at hotels like Michelberger Hotel or Hotel Indigo, offering contemporary architectural features and a trendy atmosphere.
- **Budget-Friendly Hostels:** Meet fellow travelers and share stories at hostels like Sunflower Hostel, featuring affordable dorm beds and lively common areas.
- **Ferienwohnungen (Vacation Apartments):** Rent a charming apartment in a historic building for a more local experience, offering the flexibility and comfort of your own space.
- **Airbnbs:** Discover novel living spaces and hidden gems through Airbnb, from vintage lofts to modern studios, giving you a glimpse into local life.

Whether you're a budget backpacker or a luxury seeker, Kreuzberg-Friedrichshain offers a diverse range of accommodations to suit your style and budget. Choose your haven, settle in, and prepare to explore the heartbeat of Berlin from your perfect base.

Lichtenberg: Beyond the Wall, a District Reborn

Lichtenberg, a district often overshadowed by Berlin's dynamic center, hides a rich history, a colorful culture, and surprising serenity within its borders. Once divided by the Berlin Wall, Lichtenberg embraced reunification with a quiet strength, transforming its scars into spaces of remembrance and rebirth. It's a captivating blend of historical tales, bustling markets, family-friendly fun, and hidden green havens waiting to be explored.

Historical Background

Lichtenberg's story stretches back to the 13th century when it was a mere farming village. Over time, it evolved into a center for industry and trade, attracting a diverse population. The turbulent 20th century saw Lichtenberg divided by the Berlin Wall, placing it squarely within East Germany. Today, the district proudly claims its past while embracing its newfound freedom and multicultural fabric.

Main Attractions

Lichtenberg offers a rich assortment of experiences, from immersing in history to exploring serene green havens.

- **Tierpark Berlin:** Venture on a global safari without leaving the city at Tierpark Berlin, one of Europe's largest zoos. Witness magnificent creatures from Asia to Africa, roam expansive enclosures, and discover interactive exhibits for all ages.

  As of the writing of this book, the normal opening hours are from 10 am to 8 pm from Monday to Sunday, but please always double-check the opening hours online should there have been any slight changes in their schedule.

Tierpark Berlin.
Agadez, CC BY-SA 3.0 <http://creativecommons.org/licenses/by-sa/3.0/>, via Wikimedia Commons: https://commons.wikimedia.org/wiki/File:Tierpark_Berlin_-_Main_entry.jpg

- **Stasi Museum:** Unravel the chilling secrets of the Cold War at the Stasi Museum, housed in the former headquarters of the East German secret police. Explore interactive exhibits, witness surveillance technology, and discover the stories of victims and perpetrators.

Stasi Museum.

- **Friedrichsfelde Palace:** In the heart of Berlin's Tierpark Zoo lies Friedrichsfelde Palace, a grand Neoclassical gem. Built in the 17th century, it started as a pleasure house before becoming a residence for the Prussian nobility. Today, it showcases its rich history through exhibitions. Transformed into a museum and event space, the palace now hosts classical concerts and cultural gatherings. After admiring its architecture, step outside and explore the surrounding park, where the notable Treskow family cemetery rests.

- **Hohenschönhausen Memorial:** Pay your respects and learn from the past at the Hohenschönhausen Memorial, a former Stasi prison transformed into a powerful reminder of political repression. Walk through reconstructed cells, listen to survivor testimonies, and confront the chilling realities of authoritarian regimes.

Hohenschönhausen Memorial.

- **Dong Xuan Center:** Visit a bustling marketplace at the Dong Xuan Center, home to over 1,000 stalls overflowing with exotic goods. Bargain for everything from Vietnamese delicacies and spices to souvenirs and electronics and experience a vibrant slice of Vietnamese culture.

Dong Xuan Center.

- **Friedrichsfelde Central Cemetery:** Find serenity and historical significance within the vast expanse of Friedrichsfelde Central Cemetery. Stroll through peaceful paths, discover ornate mausoleums, and pay your respects to notable figures like politicians and artists.

Friedrichsfelde Central Cemetary.

- **Rummelsburg Bay:** Unwind on the banks of the Spree River at Rummelsburg Bay. Enjoy scenic walks along the promenade, soak up the sun on the marina, or rent a boat and explore the tranquil waters.

Rummelsburg Bay.

Did You Know: Lichtenberg was home to the famous "Stasi City," the headquarters of the East German secret police, now an insightful museum.

Transport

Navigating Lichtenberg is a breeze with a variety of convenient options:

- **U-Bahn (Underground Train):** The U5 line crosses through the district, making reaching major attractions like Tierpark Berlin or the Stasi Museum easy.
- **S-Bahn (City Train):** Lines S3, S5 and S75 connect Lichtenberg to various parts of Berlin, including Mitte and Alexanderplatz.
- **Trams:** Trams offer scenic journeys through the district, connecting neighborhoods and popular landmarks.
- **Buses:** A dense network of buses covers all corners of Lichtenberg, providing flexible and affordable options.
- **Bicycles:** Explore the district at your own pace on dedicated bike lanes, offering a healthy and eco-friendly way to discover hidden gems.

Did You Know: The district boasts one of Berlin's largest parks, Tierpark Berlin, housing over 8,000 animals from across the globe.

Experiences

Lichtenberg provides experiences that go beyond the tourist trail, inviting you to discover its past and present:

- **Cold War History Tours:** Uncover the secrets of the Stasi regime with specialized tours, exploring hidden listening posts, abandoned bunkers, and historical landmarks.
- **Street Art Walks:** Get off the beaten path and discover Lichtenberg's burgeoning street art scene, encountering hidden murals, vibrant alleyways, and the stories they tell.
- **Community Events:** Join local celebrations, street festivals, and cultural gatherings to experience the spirit of Lichtenberg firsthand. Immerse yourself in Vietnamese New Year festivities at the Dong Xuan Center or browse handicrafts at the Christmas market.
- **Family Fun Days:** Explore Tierpark Berlin's interactive exhibits with your little ones, or learn about the Cold War through family-friendly tours at the Hohenschönhausen Memorial.

- **Kayaking Adventures:** Paddle down the Spree River, navigating past historical landmarks and hidden waterways, offering a rare perspective on Lichtenberg's beauty.

Did You Know: Lichtenberg is a haven for street art, with colorful murals adorning buildings and bridges, telling stories of the past and present.

Family Fun

Lichtenberg welcomes families with open arms, offering engaging activities and enchanting spaces for all ages:

- **Tierpark Berlin:** Explore fascinating animal habitats, marvel at majestic creatures, and participate in interactive family workshops at Tierpark Berlin, creating lasting memories for all ages.
- **Dong Xuan Center:** Introduce your family to Vietnamese culture through a sensory adventure at the bustling market. Sample exotic street food, explore colorful stalls, and discover colorful souvenirs.

Where to Eat

Lichtenberg's culinary scene reflects its multifaceted character, offering everything from local delights to international flavors:

- **Vietnamese Cuisine:** Explore the delicious world of Vietnamese food at the Dong Xuan Center's numerous restaurants and stalls, savoring pho noodle soups, flavorful banh mi sandwiches, and spring rolls brimming with fresh ingredients.
- **German Comfort Food:** Savor hearty Schnitzel and juicy sausages at traditional pubs. Enjoy authentic German cuisine in a warm and welcoming atmosphere.
- **Street Food Markets:** Fuel your explorations with delectable bites at Lichtenberg's street food markets, featuring international flavors from Turkish grills to Thai curries.
- **Picnics in the Park:** Pack a basket with goodies and enjoy a serene picnic in the spacious grounds of Tierpark Berlin or Rummelsburg Bay.

Did You Know: The Hohenschönhausen Memorial, a former Stasi prison, is a powerful reminder of political repression and a testament to human resilience.

Shopping Guide

Lichtenberg's shopping scene is as diverse as its residents, offering a treasure trove for bargain hunters, vintage enthusiasts, and design connoisseurs:

- **Dong Xuan Center:** Shop for everything under the sun at this vast marketplace, from Vietnamese clothing and electronics to household goods and souvenirs. Hone your bargaining skills and discover uncommon finds at every corner.

- **Second-Hand and Antique Stores:** Treasure hunters can rejoice in Lichtenberg's abundance of second-hand and antique stores like Flohmarkt Lichtenberg or Vintage & Design im Kastanienhof, unearthing hidden gems and vintage treasures.

- **Local Boutiques:** Discover rare fashion finds and handcrafted goods at independent boutiques like The Store x Berlin or SoLeMi, supporting local designers and finding pieces reflecting Lichtenberg's creative spirit.

- **Farmers' Markets:** Stock up on fresh produce, flowers, and artisanal goods at Lichtenberg's vibrant farmers' markets, held regularly in squares like Roederplatz.

- **Shopping Malls:** For a dose of modern convenience, head to the Lichtenberg Forum shopping mall, offering a variety of stores, from clothing brands to supermarkets and cafes.

- **Art and Craft Markets:** Browse for handcrafted jewelry, artwork, and handcrafted souvenirs at Lichtenberg's vibrant art and craft markets, which are held regularly at locations like Kulturhaus Karlshorst or Rummelsburger Bucht.

- **Specialty Stores:** Discover a taste of the world at Lichtenberg's specialty stores, with shops dedicated to Vietnamese ingredients at Dong Xuan Market, Turkish delights at Kaan Grill & Lebensmittel, or Polish delicacies at Sklep Polski.

Entertainment

While not boasting nightclubs like Kreuzberg, Lichtenberg offers a blend of cultural experiences and laid-back entertainment:

- **Theater and Performances:** Attend captivating shows and contemporary performances at venues like the Theater an der Parkaue or Kulturhaus Karlshorst, with everything from drama and comedy to concerts and dance recitals.

- **Live Music:** Visit quaint bars for a taste of the local music culture. Many host live bands that perform a wide range of musical styles, from jazz to indie rock.

- **Cinemas:** Watch blockbuster hits or independent gems at CineMotion Berlin Hohenschönhausen, known for its family-friendly atmosphere.

- **Bar Hopping:** Explore the district's diverse nightlife scene, hopping between trendy bars like Cocktail Bar or Alibi, enjoying cocktails, catching live music, or soaking up the lively atmosphere.

- **Cultural Events:** Soak up the Lichtenberg culture with themed events, festivals, and celebrations throughout the year. Enjoy Vietnamese New Year festivities at the Dong Xuan Center, or participate in community art workshops.

Did You Know: Lichtenberg vibrates with international flavors, hosting the largest Vietnamese market in Europe, the Dong Xuan Center.

Sports and Leisure

Lichtenberg provides ample opportunities for active pursuits and serene relaxation:

- **Cycling:** Explore the district on two wheels in dedicated bike lanes, follow the Spree River, or venture into Tierpark Berlin.

- **Swimming:** Take a refreshing dip in the historic Stadtbad Lichtenberg, featuring indoor and outdoor pools, or enjoy water sports like kayaking or paddleboarding on the Spree River.

- **Hiking and Jogging:** Lace up your shoes and explore the green havens of Rummelsburg Bay or Tiergarten, offering scenic trails and peaceful escapes.

- **Yoga and Fitness:** Unwind and recharge at studios like Yoga Loft Lichtenberg or Lichtenberg Sports Club, offering diverse yoga classes, meditation sessions, and gym facilities.

- **Boat Trips:** Enjoy a leisurely cruise on the Spree River, offering a different perspective on Lichtenberg's landmarks and beautiful scenery.

Accommodations

Lichtenberg has a range of accommodation options for every budget and travel style:

- **Budget-Friendly Hostels:** Meet fellow travelers and share stories at hostels like the a&o Hostel Berlin Kolumbus or Jugendherberger Berlin Ostkreuz, providing affordable dorm beds, vibrant common areas, and a social atmosphere.
- **Ferienwohnungen (Vacation Apartments):** Rent a charming apartment like those at Lichtenberg Apartmenthaus for a more local experience, offering the flexibility and comfort of your own space.
- **Airbnbs:** Discover exciting living spaces and hidden gems through Airbnb, from vintage lofts to modern studios, giving you a glimpse into the heart of Lichtenberg's neighborhoods.

Berlin's Kreuzberg-Friedrichshain is a buzzing blend of art, history, and nightlife. Street art murals splash across vibrant streets while trendy cafes hum with conversation. Music venues thrum with alternative beats and history is etched in every corner. Lichtenberg offers a calmer counterpart to Berlin's energy. Green parks like Tiergarten Lichtenberg invite peaceful strolls, while history is evident in the neighborhoods. These diverse districts promise a blend of urban ease and quiet escapes, perfect for those seeking a relaxing Berlin experience.

Chapter 5: Neukölln – Tempelhof-Schöneberg

Berlin's southern sprawl embraces two distinct districts of Neukölln and Tempelhof-Schöneberg. As diverse as they are captivating, each boasts a remarkable history, culture, and community. Neukölln, the gritty phoenix rising from a complex past, ticks with youthful energy and artistic expression. Its streets speak tales of resilience and transformation, while its lively markets and eclectic eateries offer a glimpse into a kaleidoscope of cultures.

Across the border, Tempelhof-Schöneberg unveils a contrasting charm. Grand avenues draped in history lead to the sprawling Tempelhofer Feld, a verdant oasis where the ghosts of planes once soared. Yet, a bohemian spirit takes flight within its elegant facades and leafy parks, drawing artists and intellectuals to its cafes and galleries. It's time to uncover these districts one at a time.

Neukölln: Embracing Grit and Glam

Neukölln, a district in Berlin renowned for its resonant artistic scene, gritty charm, and evolving identity, thumps with a life all its own. Once considered a rough-around-the-edges neighborhood, it has blossomed into a melting pot of cultures, where historical relics rub shoulders with trendy cafes and avant-garde galleries. This section will unravel the layers of Neukölln, giving you a glimpse into its past, present, and endless possibilities for exploration.

Historical Background

Neukölln's story stretches back centuries, its first mention dating to 1237. From a rural village to a Prussian industrial hub, it experienced rapid growth in the 19th century. The Second World War left its scars, and subsequent decades saw economic struggles and social challenges. However, the fall of the Berlin Wall in 1989 ushered in a new era of transformation. Artists and creative minds, drawn by its affordable rents and character, injected their energy into the district, laying the foundation for its current renaissance.

Main Attractions

With its dynamic spirit and endless possibilities, Neukölln beckons you to explore its vivaciousness.

- **Schloss Britz:** Immerse yourself in the opulent luxury of the 18th-century Britz Palace and its enchanting gardens. Stroll through the manicured lawns, explore the orangery, and relive the grandeur of aristocratic life.

  As of the writing of this book, the normal opening hours are from 12 pm to 6 pm from Tuesday to Sunday, but please always double-check the opening hours online should there have been any slight changes in their schedule.

Schloss Britz.
A.Savin, FAL, via Wikimedia Commons.
https://commons.wikimedia.org/wiki/File:Berlin_Britz_Schloss_asv2021-03_img2.jpg

- **Britzer Garten:** Escape the urban symphony into the haven of Britzer Garten. Cycle along idyllic paths. Rent a boat on the lake or picnic amid the beautiful array of flowers. This sprawling park is a breath of fresh air for all ages.

As of the writing of this book, the normal opening hours are from 9 am to 6 pm from Monday to Sunday, but please always double-check the opening hours online should there have been any slight changes in their schedule.

Britzer Garten.
RKG1H, CC BY-SA 3.0 <https://creativecommons.org/licenses/by-sa/3.0>, via Wikimedia Commons. https://commons.wikimedia.org/wiki/File:Britzer_garten_im_see.JPG

- **Maybachufer and Turkish Market:** Soak up the lively atmosphere of the Maybachufer. Browse the vibrant stalls of the Tuesday and Friday Turkish Market, tantalizing your senses with exotic spices, traditional textiles, and mouthwatering street food.

As of the writing of this book, the normal opening hours are from 12 pm to 6:30 pm from Monday to Sunday, but please always double-check the opening hours online should there have been any slight changes in their schedule.

Maybachufer and Turkish Market.

- **Körnerpark:** Discover a slice of tranquility in the heart of Neukölln. Wander through the meticulously landscaped gardens, admire the classical sculptures, and find solace in the serene ambiance of the historic orangery.

You can visit any time you want.

Körnerpark.

Frank Schubert, CC BY-SA 4.0 <https://creativecommons.org/licenses/by-sa/4.0>, via Wikimedia Commons. https://commons.wikimedia.org/wiki/File:K%C3%B6rnerpark0047.jpg

- **Richardplatz:** Step back in time at the charming Richardplatz. Browse the quaint shops, savor traditional German fare at a cozy restaurant, and uncover the district's history at the Rixdorf Museum.

  You can visit any time you want.

Richardplatz.

Fridolin freudenfett, CC BY-SA 4.0 <https://creativecommons.org/licenses/by-sa/4.0>, via Wikimedia Commons. https://commons.wikimedia.org/wiki/File:Neuk%C3%B6lln_Richardplatz-002.jpg

- **Neuköllner Opera:** Be captivated by the cultural Neuköllner Opera. This historic theater promises an enriching experience, from contemporary dance performances and classical concerts to thought-provoking exhibitions.

  There are no fixed hours, so check their website: https://www.neukoellneroper.de/en/schedule/ for accurate times and dates.

- **Hufeisensiedlung:** Lose yourself in the world of "Berlin Modernism" at the UNESCO-listed Hufeisensiedlung. Explore the horseshoe-shaped complex of colorful houses, marvel at the innovative design, and appreciate the enduring legacy of this architectural movement.

You can visit any time you want.

Hufeisensiedlung.

Rainer Halama, CC BY-SA 4.0 <https://creativecommons.org/licenses/by-sa/4.0>, via Wikimedia Commons. https://commons.wikimedia.org/wiki/File:WLM-DE-BE-2018-Britz-Hufeisensiedlung-4190.jpg

Did You Know: Designed by Bruno Taut and Martin Wagner, the Hufeisensiedlung is a masterpiece of early modernist architecture.

Transport

Getting around Neukölln is a breeze. The U7 subway line serves several prominent stops within the district, while numerous bus routes offer flexible connections. Cycling remains a popular choice, with dedicated lanes and rental stations readily available. Taxis are always an option. But consider venturing along the Landwehr Canal by boat for a scenic adventure.

Experiences

From historical gems to artistic hotbeds and trendy cafes to family-friendly parks, Neukölln offers a kaleidoscope of experiences for every traveler.

- **Street Art Tours:** Uncover the hidden gems of Neukölln's thriving street art scene. These tours are led by local experts, introduce you to talented artists, explore new and exciting styles, and peek into the city's contemporary culture.

- **Foodie Trails:** Embark on a culinary adventure through Neukölln's diverse culinary landscape. Sample everything from traditional Turkish pide and mouthwatering Vietnamese pho to trendy vegan cafes and hidden-gem tapas bars.

- **Alternative Berlin Tours:** Go beyond the tourist facade and discover the authentic Neukölln experience. Discover the vibrant LGBTQ+ scene, explore underground music venues, and taste the district's rebellious spirit.

Did You Know: David Bowie famously resided in Neukölln in the 1970s, drawing inspiration for his iconic album "Heroes" from the divided city.

Family Fun

- **Kinderbauernhof Britz:** Let your little ones connect with nature at the Kinderbauernhof Britz. This charming working farm allows children to feed goats, cuddle rabbits, and learn about farm life through interactive activities.

- **Neukölln Arcaden:** Escape the rain at the Neukölln Arcaden. This family-friendly shopping center offers a mix of children's clothing stores, toy shops, and a cinema, keeping everyone entertained for an afternoon.

Where to Eat

Neukölln's culinary scene is a melting pot of flavors, reflecting its diverse cultural heritage.

- **Turkish Delights:** Satisfy your cravings for authentic Turkish cuisine at Gel Gor, Gozleme, or Berlin Tantuni. Dig into succulent kebabs, savory pide, and heartwarming stews, savoring the rich spices and traditional recipes.

- **Hipster Hangouts:** Immerse yourself in the trendy Neukölln vibe at Muted Horn or Klunkerkranich. Enjoy brunch delights, craft cocktails, and an atmosphere fueled by creative energy.

- **Hidden Gems:** Seek out Neukölln's culinary treasures. You'll find hidden gems tucked away on side streets, like Vin Aqua Vin or Prachtwerk.

Did You Know: The Rixdorf Museum boasts the oldest wooden house in Berlin, dating back to 1737.

Shopping Guide

Neukölln's shopping scene is as varied as its residents, with a mix of vintage treasures, independent boutiques, and local markets.

- **Vintage Paradise:** Dive into the treasure trove of Neukölln's vintage stores. Stöberhalle, Scherben Glück, and Rummelszirkus Berlin offer a curated selection of clothing, furniture, and homeware, with unusual finds for every taste.

- **Independent Boutiques:** Discover the creative spirit of Neukölln at independent boutiques like Voo Store, NVA Berlin, and Atelier am Mauerpark. Pick up locally-made jewelry, handcrafted accessories, and one-of-a-kind art pieces.

- **Outdoor Markets:** Soak up the beautiful atmosphere of Neukölln's street markets. On Sundays, Schmöckernmarkt has an array of vintage clothing, antiques, and delicious street food. On Tuesdays and Fridays, the Turkish Market bursts with colors and aromas.

- **Record Stores:** Unearth musical gems at Neukölln's independent record stores. Groove to vinyl classics at Oye Records, browse the eclectic selection at Dodo, or find rare finds at Plattenläden im Bergmannkiez.

Entertainment

Neukölln's nightlife pulsates with an eclectic mix of music, film, and theater.

- **Independent Cinema:** Experience independent cinema at Neukölln's theaters. Attend film screenings and discussions at Passage or catch underground flicks at Moviemento.

- **Theater and Performance:** Witness innovative and thought-provoking productions at Neukölln's vibrant theater scene. Immerse yourself in the experimental performances at Heimathafen Neukölln or be captivated by shows at the Neukölln Oper.

Did You Know: Neukölln is home to the largest Turkish community in Germany, contributing to its rich culture.

Sports and Leisure

Neukölln is a haven for those seeking active pursuits and relaxed moments.

- **Outdoor Adventures:** Cycle along the scenic Landwehr Canal, rent a boat for a tranquil exploration, or jog through the lush expanses of Britzer Garten.
- **Fitness and Wellbeing:** Rejuvenate your mind and body at Neukölln's diverse fitness studios. Practice yoga at Dharma Yoga or sweat it out at Studio 49.
- **Green Retreats:** Seek solace in Neukölln's tranquil green spaces. Pack a picnic basket and unwind in Körnerpark, bask in the sun at Tempelhofer Feld, or explore the verdant paths of Hasenheide Park.

Did You Know: The Maybachufer and its surrounding area was a bustling port until the early 20th century.

Accommodations

Neukölln offers a variety of accommodations to suit all budgets and tastes.

- **Boutique Hotels:** Experience Neukölln's trendy vibe at hotels like Leonardo Boutique Hotel, with its sleek design, or Hüttenpalast, with its retro-style caravans and cabins located within an indoor camping site inside two old factory halls.
- **Budget-Friendly Options:** Find affordable comfort at hostels like Grand Hostel Berlin Urban or 2A Hostel Berlin. Meet fellow travelers, participate in social events, and explore the city on a shoestring budget.

Additional Tips:

- Learn basic German phrases to enhance your experience and connect with locals.
- Purchase a Berlin Welcome Card for discounted public transportation and access to museums and attractions.
- Pack comfortable shoes for exploring the district on foot.
- Consider renting a bike for a more flexible and eco-friendly way to get around.
- Be open to the unexpected and let Neukölln's charm surprise you.

Neukölln is a district that defies definition, constantly evolving and surprising its visitors. Embrace the grit and glam of this captivating district, wander its streets, discover hidden treasures, and create your own Neukölln adventure.

Tempelhof-Schöneberg: Where History Meets Hipster in Berlin

Tempelhof-Schöneberg is a district in Berlin with a dynamic medley of historical grandeur and contemporary cool. This district offers a sensory overload for every traveler, from the sprawling expanse of Tempelhofer Feld to the elegant shops of KaDeWe. Buckle up because you're about to dive into the fiery heart of Tempelhof-Schöneberg and discover its hidden gems, historical backdrop, and modern buzz.

Historical Background

Tempelhof and Schöneberg, once separate districts, merged in 2001, bringing together their tumultuous histories. Named after the Knights Templar, who resided there in the 13th century, Tempelhof became a military airfield in the 20th century, witnessing pivotal moments like the Berlin Airlift. With its grand architecture and bohemian spirit, Schöneberg was a hub of artistic and political movements, becoming the LGBTQ+ center of West Berlin after World War II. Today, the combined district proudly embraces its past, showcasing historical landmarks, trendy cafes, and cutting-edge art.

Did You Know: John F. Kennedy's iconic "Ich bin ein Berliner" speech was delivered at the Schöneberg Town Hall in 1963, solidifying the district's symbolic importance.

Main Attractions

- **Tempelhofer Feld:** This sprawling former airfield is a paradise for outdoor enthusiasts. Hike, bike, swim, picnic, or simply soak up the sun in this vast urban oasis. Don't miss the iconic hangars, remnants of the airport's past.

  As of the writing of this book, the normal opening hours are from 6 am to 7 pm from Monday to Sunday, but please always double-check the opening hours online should there have been any slight changes in their schedule.

Tempelhofer Feld.
A.Savin, FAL, via Wikimedia Commons:
https://commons.wikimedia.org/wiki/File:Berlin_Tempelhofer_Feld_asv2019-09_img3.jpg

- **KaDeWe - Kaufhaus des Westens:** Prepare for intensive retail therapy at this renowned department store. Lose yourself in the luxury brands, indulge in gourmet delights on the top floors, and admire the opulent Art Deco architecture.

As of the writing of this book, the normal opening hours are from 10 am to 8 pm from Monday to Thursday and Saturday and 10 am to 9 pm on Friday. Please always double-check the opening hours online should there have been any slight changes in their schedule.

KaDeWe.

Jörg Zägel, CC BY-SA 3.0 <https://creativecommons.org/licenses/by-sa/3.0>, via Wikimedia Commons: https://commons.wikimedia.org/wiki/File:Berlin,_Schoeneberg,_Tauentzienstrasse_21-24,_KaDeWe.jpg

- **Schöneberg Town Hall:** Stand on the podium where John F. Kennedy delivered his historic speech, "Ich bin ein Berliner," and relive a famous moment in Berlin's history. Explore the building's interior and learn about the district's rich political and cultural heritage.

As of the writing of this book, the normal opening hours are from 8 am to 3 pm on Monday and Wednesday, 10 am to 6 pm on Tuesday and Thursday, and 8 am to 1 pm on Friday, but please always double-check the opening hours online should there have been any slight changes in their schedule.

Schöneberg Town Hall.
A.Savin, FAL, via Wikimedia Commons:
https://commons.wikimedia.org/wiki/File:Berlin_Rathaus_Sch%C3%B6neberg_asv2021-06.jpg

- **Viktoria-Luise-Platz:** Embrace the charm of this elegant square. Sip coffee at a cafe, watch the world go by, and admire the surrounding historical buildings. Don't miss the ornate fountain and the nearby local produce and craft market.

  You can visit any time you want.

Viktoria-Luise Platz.

- **Urban Nation:** Admire the street art at this open-air gallery. Witness the ever-changing canvas of murals, from local artists to international stars, and discover the beautiful pulse of Berlin's street art scene.

  You can visit any time you want.

Urban Nation.
Singlespeedfahrer, CC0, via Wikimedia Commons:
https://commons.wikimedia.org/wiki/File:Urban_Nation_Museum_Berlin.jpg

- **Schöneberger Südgelände Nature Park:** Step into an unexpected urban oasis. Explore the abandoned railway tracks transformed into natural trails, discover art installations hidden among the greenery, and enjoy a blend of industrial and natural beauty.

As of the writing of this book, the normal opening hours are from 9 am to 6 pm from Monday to Sunday, but please always double-check the opening hours online should there have been any slight changes in their schedule.

Schöneberger Südgelände Nature Park.
Jacobo.ka, CC BY-SA 4.0 <https://creativecommons.org/licenses/by-sa/4.0>, via Wikimedia Commons: https://commons.wikimedia.org/wiki/File:0016-_1LCP_Natur-Park_Sch%C3%B6neberger_S%C3%BCdgel%C3%A4nde,_Berlin.jpg

Did You Know: Marlene Dietrich, the legendary actress, once lived in Schöneberg, and her former apartment is now a historical landmark.

Transport

Tempelhof-Schöneberg has excellent public transport options.

- **U-Bahn (Underground):** Lines U7, U4, U1, and U2 provide excellent connectivity with other parts of Berlin.

- **S-Bahn (Suburban Trains):** Schöneberg, Priesterweg, and Südkreuz stations connect you to regional hubs.

- **Buses:** Numerous bus lines crisscross the district, offering convenient access to local attractions.

- **Bikes:** Rental stations abound, making this a perfect way to explore Tempelhofer Feld and other green spaces.
- **Walking:** For the curious and courageous, exploring on foot is a great way to stumble upon hidden gems.

Experiences

Tempelhof-Schöneberg is about immersing yourself in the district's vibe:

- **Cold War Tour:** Take a guided walk through history, retracing the footsteps of iconic figures and exploring Cold War landmarks.
- **Street Art Safari:** Join a tour or undertake your own adventure with a curated map, or let your eyes guide you as you discover the ever-evolving canvas of Urban Nation and beyond.
- **Foodie Tour:** Dive into the district's varied culinary scene, sampling local specialties like currywurst and schnitzel or discovering international flavors at KaDeWe's gourmet food hall.
- **Christmas Markets (Seasonal):** During the festive season, captivate yourself with the magic of Berlin's Christmas markets, sip on Glühwein (mulled wine), and browse for handcrafted ornaments at Nollendorfplatz.

Did You Know: The Bauhaus-inspired Königin-Luise-Kirche in Tempelhof is one of the few surviving examples of church architecture from the interwar period.

Family Fun

Tempelhof-Schöneberg caters to families of all shapes and sizes:

- **Tempelhofer Feld:** With its vast open spaces, playgrounds, and bike paths, this urban oasis is a paradise for kids to run wild and explore. Pack a picnic basket and enjoy a family day out in the sunshine.
- **Schöneberger Südgelände Nature Park:** Let imaginations run wild in this nature haven, where kids can spot butterflies, climb wooden structures, and discover hidden treasures amongst the greenery.

Where to Eat

Tempelhof-Schöneberg tantalizes your taste buds, from Michelin-starred restaurants to cozy cafes and bustling street food stalls:

- **Bonivant Cocktail Bistro:** This restaurant offers a vegetarian-vegan experience with a balance of expertise and experimentation. Indulge in some of the best dishes in the area.
- **Mezban:** For a little international flavor, visit Mezban and indulge in some of the finest Indian dishes in Berlin. Offering a mix of the greatest Indian flavors, guests are promised a wonderful experience.
- **Nollendorfplatz:** This beautiful square is a haven for international eats, with Vietnamese pho, Turkish pide, and Italian pasta within walking distance.
- **Tempelhofer Feld Food Stalls:** On sunny days, the Feld comes alive with food stalls offering everything from burgers and falafel to vegan wraps and ice cream. Perfect for a casual picnic lunch.

Did You Know: The Urban Nation Street art gallery in Schöneberg boasts the world's largest street art mural, created by Berlin-based artist Ememem.

Shopping Guide

From designer labels to vintage finds and local crafts, Tempelhof-Schöneberg is a shopper's paradise:

- **KaDeWe – Kaufhaus des Westens:** Ascend the escalators of this luxury department store and prepare to be dazzled by designer fashion, gourmet food, and homeware.
- **Nollendorfplatz:** Browse antique shops, quirky independent stores, and LGBTQ+ bookstores around this lively square, where quirky finds are just around the corner.
- **Schöneberg Market:** Held every Tuesday and Friday, this open-air market is a treasure trove of fresh produce, handmade crafts, and local delicacies.
- **Tempelhofer Feld Flea Market (Sundays):** Hunt for vintage gems, furniture, and clothing at this sprawling flea market, where bargains and surprises abound.

Sports and Leisure

Whether you're a fitness enthusiast or simply seeking recreational activities, Tempelhof-Schöneberg has something for you:

- **Tempelhofer Feld:** Hike, bike, skate, swim, or play sports in this vast urban oasis. Join a yoga class on the lawn, rent a boat on the lagoon, or simply stretch out under the sun.

- **Schöneberger Südgelände Nature Park:** Go cycling or mountain biking on the dedicated trails, jog among the greenery, or join a guided birdwatching tour to discover the park's hidden wildlife.

- **Schöneberg Aquatic Center:** Dive into indoor and outdoor pools, take a fitness class, or relax in the sauna at this modern aquatic complex.

Did You Know: Once a military airfield, Tempelhofer Feld is now Europe's largest urban park and a green haven for Berliners.

Accommodations

Tempelhof-Schöneberg caters to all budgets and preferences with its accommodation options:

- **Luxury Hotels:** Immerse yourself in opulent comfort at Hotel Schöneberg. Spacious rooms, impeccable service, and a prime location make it a perfect choice for the discerning traveler. To experience impeccable service and luxurious amenities, book a stay at LINDEMANN'S. This hotel is perfect for those seeking an indulgent stay.

- **Budget Options:** The Niu Dwarf Hotel boasts industrial-chic rooms and a quirky art collection. This stylish and modern hotel offers compact yet perfectly designed rooms at an affordable price. Perfect for budget-conscious travelers who still appreciate a touch of design.

- **AirBnB:** Tempelhof-Schöneberg boasts a wide selection of AirBnB listings, from cozy apartments to stylish lofts.

As you conclude your exploration of Neukölln and Tempelhof-Schöneberg, you've learned a new respect and a deeper understanding of their charm and undeniable appeal. Whether you're drawn to Neukölln's edgy energy or Tempelhof-Schöneberg's historical elegance, these districts are a glimpse into the heart and soul of Berlin. So, go forth and explore, wander through hidden alleys, savor the local flavors, and discover your favorite corners of these captivating Berlin districts.

Chapter 6: Steglitz-Zehlendorf – Spandau

Beyond the clamor of Berlin's central core, Steglitz-Zehlendorf and Spandau present a different melody. Steeped in history, adorned with cultural riches, and sprinkled with natural wonders, these districts are an alluring escape from the urban rhythm. From the gilded halls of Cecilienhof Palace to the starlit expanse of Grunewald Forest, each corner tells a forgotten tale.

Whether you seek the grandeur of Prussian palaces, the tranquility of lakeside havens, or the thrill of Berlin's lesser-known gems, Steglitz-Zehlendorf and Spandau hold something enchanting for every traveler's heart. So, grab your camera and let your curiosity guide you. In these captivating districts, hidden jewels await, promising to leave you enchanted and hungry for more.

Steglitz-Zehlendorf

Steglitz-Zehlendorf, a district in the southwest of Berlin, welcomes you with a strange blend of historical charm, cultural offerings, and serene natural beauty. From the elegant streets of Steglitz to the verdant landscapes of Zehlendorf, this diverse district unveils stories of Prussian grandeur, artistic expression, and modern urban life.

Historical Background

Once separate villages, Steglitz and Zehlendorf boast rich and distinct histories. Founded in the 13th century, Steglitz thrived as a trading hub and later became a fashionable residential area for Berlin's elite. On the other hand, Zehlendorf, with its aristocratic roots and proximity to the Grunewald forest, was favored by Prussian nobility and artists. In 1920, these two distinct entities merged to form the district of Steglitz-Zehlendorf, retaining their identities while creating a harmonious whole.

Main Attractions

- **Botanischer Garten und Botanisches Museum:** Transplant yourself into botanical wonders at the extensive Botanical Garden, housing flora from around the globe. Explore the accompanying museum and uncover the fascinating realm of plant life.

  As of the writing of this book, the normal opening hours are from 9 am to 8 pm from Monday to Sunday, but please always double-check the opening hours online should there have been any slight changes in their schedule.

Botanisches Museum.
Axel Mauruszat, Attribution, via Wikimedia Commons.
https://commons.wikimedia.org/wiki/File:2006-08-20_Botanisches_Museum.jpg

- **Schlossstraße:** Indulge in a shopping spree on this iconic avenue, browsing through designer boutiques, department stores like KaDeWe's smaller sibling, and charming cafes.

You can visit any time you want.

Schlossstraße.

Dguendel, CC BY 3.0 <https://creativecommons.org/licenses/by/3.0>, via Wikimedia Commons.
https://commons.wikimedia.org/wiki/File:Berlin-Steglitz,_Haus_Schlossstra%C3%9Fe_27.jpg

- **Haus am Waldsee:** Discover contemporary art amid the serene beauty of the Grunewald forest. This lakeside gallery offers a colorful blend of artistic expression and natural tranquility.

As of the writing of this book, the normal opening hours are from 11 am to 6 pm from Tuesday to Sunday, but please always double-check the opening hours online should there have been any slight changes in their schedule.

Haus am Waldsee.
Haus am Waldsee, CC BY-SA 4.0 <https://creativecommons.org/licenses/by-sa/4.0>, via Wikimedia Commons.
https://commons.wikimedia.org/wiki/File:Haus_am_Waldsee_Internationale_Kunst_in_Berlin,_20 19,_Foto_Bernd_Borchardt.jpg

- **Krumme Lanke:** Escape the city's bustle and bask in the picturesque charm of this lake. Enjoy a picnic on the shores, stroll around, or rent a boat and explore the tranquil waters.

You can visit any time you want.

Krumme Lanke.

Lukas Beck, CC BY-SA 4.0 <https://creativecommons.org/licenses/by-sa/4.0>, via Wikimedia Commons. https://commons.wikimedia.org/wiki/File:Berlin_Krumme_Lanke.jpg

- **Steglitzer Stadtpark:** Find your green haven in this local park, which is perfect for families and nature lovers. Playgrounds, walking paths, and lush greenery offer a welcome respite from the urban landscape.

You can visit any time you want.

- **Pfaueninsel:** Unwind on this enchanting island, a UNESCO World Heritage Site adorned with historical charm and natural beauty. Visit the fairytale-like Pfaueninsel Castle, explore the Dairy Cottage, and wander through picturesque gardens.

As of the writing of this book, the normal opening hours are from 10 am to 6 pm on Monday and Sunday, but please always double-check the opening hours online should there have been any slight changes in their schedule.

Pfaueninsel.

Georgfotoart, CC BY-SA 4.0 <https://creativecommons.org/licenses/by-sa/4.0>, via Wikimedia Commons. https://commons.wikimedia.org/wiki/File:Meierei-Wirtschaftshof_(Pfaueninsel)_01.jpg

Transport

With its efficient public transport network and diverse options, getting around Steglitz-Zehlendorf is easy and enjoyable.

- **U-Bahn (Underground):** Lines U7, U9, and U2 provide convenient access to various parts of the district and beyond.
- **S-Bahn (Suburban Trains):** Stations like Zehlendorf, Düppel, and Schlachtensee connect you to regional hubs.
- **Buses:** Numerous bus lines crisscross the district, providing easy access to local attractions and neighborhoods.
- **Bikes:** Rental stations abound, making exploring the green spaces and charming streets a breeze.
- **Boats:** Take a scenic boat tour on the Havel River for a comfortable perspective of the district and Pfaueninsel.

Did You Know: Albert Einstein lived in Steglitz briefly in 1915, working on his theory of general relativity.

Experiences

Steglitz-Zehlendorf offers more than just sightseeing. It's about immersing yourself in its trendy atmosphere:

- **History Tour:** Follow in the footsteps of Prussian royalty and artistic pioneers on a guided walk through Steglitz and Zehlendorf, uncovering hidden gems and fascinating stories.
- **Art and Culture Crawl:** Explore the gorgeous art scene, from contemporary galleries like Haus am Waldsee to the renowned Dahlem Museums Complex, and discover hidden artistic treasures in unexpected corners.
- **Culinary Adventure:** Journey through the district, savoring local delicacies at traditional taverns, indulging in international flavors at Schlossstraße's restaurants, or picnicking among the greenery.
- **Nature Walk:** Lace up your shoes and explore the Grunewald forest, a sprawling green oasis teeming with hiking trails, cycling paths, and hidden lakes. Breathe in the fresh air, spot local wildlife, and find your inner peace in the verdant expanse.
- **Festival Fun:** Soak up the lively atmosphere at one of Steglitz-Zehlendorf's many festivals, from the mouthwatering street festivals in summer to the charming Christmas markets in winter. Enjoy live music, local crafts, and delectable treats in a festive atmosphere.
- **Boat Trip:** Embrace the tranquility of the Havel River on a scenic boat tour. Glide past Pfaueninsel, admire the picturesque waterfront, and enjoy an uninterrupted perspective of the district's natural beauty.

Did You Know: The Grunewald forest, a beloved green oasis in Zehlendorf, was once a hunting ground for Prussian royalty.

Family Fun

Steglitz-Zehlendorf offers a delightful mix of outdoor adventures, historical explorations, and a touch of whimsy, perfect for a family day out.

- **Pfaueninsel (Peacock Island):** Take a ferry to this enchanting island, where you can explore a Prussian fairytale that has come to life. Spot free-roaming peacocks, wander through the romantic park and castle grounds, and let the kids burn off energy in the playground.
- **Steglitzer Stadtpark:** Let the kids run wild on the playgrounds, enjoy a relaxed picnic on the lawn, or take a family bike ride through the park's shady paths.

- **Strandbad Wannsee (Lake Shore Swimming Area):** Enjoy a day at the beach, Berlin style. Strandbad Wannsee boasts a vast stretch of golden sand along the shores of Wannsee, Europe's largest lake within a city. Take a refreshing dip, build sandcastles, rent a paddleboat, or simply relax and soak up the sun.
- **Domäne Dahlem:** Step back in time at this sprawling organic farm. Kids will love meeting the farmyard animals, watching blacksmith demonstrations, and learning about agriculture through interactive exhibits at the museum. Don't miss a delicious meal made with fresh, local ingredients at the on-site restaurant.
- **Pfaueninsel:** Pack a picnic basket and explore this fairytale-like island as a family. Discover the charming castle, spot peacocks roaming freely, and let your imagination run wild in the picturesque gardens.

Where to Eat

Steglitz-Zehlendorf caters to diverse palates, offering a range of dining options to suit your mood and cravings.

- **Waldhaus Zehlendorf (Beer Garden):** Soak up the sunshine and lively atmosphere at this classic Berlin beer garden. Waldhaus Zehlendorf is perfect for a casual meal with hearty German fare, refreshing drinks, and a spacious outdoor seating area ideal for families.
- **AVUS-Treff Spinner-Brücke (Austrian Restaurant):** Calling all fans of schnitzel and strudel. AVUS-Treff Spinner-Brücke offers a taste of Austria with a menu featuring traditional dishes like Wiener Schnitzel and Goulash. The restaurant is a popular spot for motorcyclists, adding a unique touch to the ambiance.
- **Osteria del Sud (Italian Restaurant):** Transport yourself to Italy with a delightful meal at Osteria del Sud. This restaurant serves up authentic Italian cuisine, from wood-fired pizzas and fresh pasta to flavorful secondi (main courses). Enjoy a cozy and intimate dining experience, perfect for a date night or a special family occasion.

Did You Know: The Pfaueninsel, a UNESCO World Heritage Site, was gifted by King Frederick William II to his mistress, Countess Wilhelmine von Lichtenau.

Shopping Guide

Steglitz-Zehlendorf is a shopper's paradise for every taste and budget, from high-end fashion and local crafts to vintage finds and everyday essentials.

- **Zehlendorfer Welle:** This modern shopping mall features a wide range of popular fashion brands, electronics stores, and department stores. It's a one-stop shop for all your shopping needs, with plenty of cafes and restaurants to fuel your retail therapy session.

- **Onkel Toms Ladenstraße:** This charming shopping mall offers a more traditional feel with a mix of local boutiques, independent shops, and familiar brand names. You'll find a good selection of clothing, gifts, and homewares here.

- **Netto Marken-Discount:** Looking to stretch your budget? Netto Marken-Discount is a popular discount supermarket chain in Germany. Here, you'll find a wide variety of groceries, household products, and everyday essentials at competitive prices. It's a great option for stocking up on supplies or grabbing a quick and affordable meal.

Entertainment

While nightlife may not be the district's main draw, Steglitz-Zehlendorf offers entertainment options for those seeking a cultural evening or a cozy night in:

- **Cineplex Titania:** Immerse yourself in the magic of cinema at the iconic Cineplex Titania. This historic Art Deco movie theater, originally built in 1928, boasts a grand atmosphere and modern amenities. Catch the latest blockbusters or discover independent gems on the big screen.

- **Schlosspark Theater:** Step back in time at the enchanting Schlosspark Theater. This early-1900s theater offers a captivating program of live performances, including concerts, plays, readings, and other performing arts events. The intimate setting and historic ambiance make it a unique and memorable experience.

- **Capitol Dahlem:** Explore the unique Capitol Dahlem, a former cinema transformed into a multi-purpose event space. The venue hosts a variety of events, from concerts and movie screenings to talks and exhibitions. Check their program for upcoming attractions that pique your interest.

Did You Know: The Botanical Garden boasts over 22,000 plant species, making it one of Europe's largest and most diverse.

Sports and Leisure

From exploring the vast Grunewald to enjoying water sports on Krumme Lanke, Steglitz-Zehlendorf provides ample opportunities for an active and healthy lifestyle.

- **Schwimmhalle Finckensteinallee:** This public swimming pool features a lap pool, perfect for a refreshing workout or practicing your strokes. It also caters to families with designated areas for children.

- **Cole-Sports-Center:** This comprehensive sports complex offers a variety of facilities for an invigorating workout. Whether you prefer group fitness classes, hitting the tennis courts, or playing badminton, Cole-Sports-Center has something for everyone.

- **EMS Training Fitbox Berlin Clayallee:** Experience a revolutionary approach to fitness with EMS (electrical muscle stimulation) training at Fitbox Berlin Clayallee. This innovative studio utilizes electric impulses to maximize your workout efficiency, offering a time-saving and effective way to achieve your fitness goals.

Did You Know: Schlossstraße, with its opulent shops and department stores, was once dubbed the "Fifth Avenue of Berlin."

Accommodations

Whether you're seeking a luxurious retreat, a trendy base for exploring, or a budget-friendly option, Steglitz-Zehlendorf has the perfect accommodation for your needs.

- **Hotel Steglitz International:** Friendly rooms and suites with free Wi-Fi and minibars, plus a cocktail bar, restaurant, and smoker's lounge. 4-star hotel.

- **Motel und Rasthof Grunewald:** Bright rooms with free Wi-Fi and parking in a casual hotel with a restaurant and bar. 3-star hotel.

- **Hotel Landhaus Schlachtensee:** Simple rooms with cable TV in a friendly hotel with Wi-Fi, parking, and breakfast. 3-star hotel.

- **Seminaris Campus Hotel Berlin:** Modern hotel in a glass-walled building with understated rooms, a restaurant, and a bar.

Beyond the must-see attractions, Steglitz-Zehlendorf holds countless hidden gems waiting to be discovered. Wander down cobbled streets to find a secret cafe, venture deeper into the forest to stumble upon a hidden lake, or lose yourself in the bustling local markets. This district rewards the curious, offering endless opportunities to create your own fantastic Berlin adventure.

Spandau

Spandau, often considered the forgotten jewel of Berlin, is a district steeped in history, brimming with vibrant life, and nestled in serene natural beauty. From the imposing walls of the Spandau Citadel to the charming cobbled streets of Altstadt Spandau, it invites peaceful exploration and surprises with unexpected modern flourishes. So, ditch the city center crowds and journey through Spandau, where time seems to bend, and every corner unfolds a new story.

Historical Background

Spandau boasts a rich and turbulent history, older than Berlin. Founded in 1197, it was a crucial trade center and strategically fortified town. The imposing Spandau Citadel, erected in the 16th century, is a testament to its military past, witnessing wars and revolutions and even housing prisoners like Rudolf Hess during World War II. Yet, beyond the battles and turmoil, Spandau thrived as a flourishing artistic and cultural center, attracting painters, musicians, and intellectuals who added their influences to the cityscape.

Main Attractions

- **Spandau Citadel (Zitadelle Spandau):** Drench yourself in the imposing presence of this Renaissance fortress, exploring its ramparts, dungeons, and museums. Learn about its fascinating history, take a guided tour, or enjoy a concert in the atmospheric courtyard.

  As of the writing of this book, the normal opening hours are from 10 am to 5 pm every day, except on Thursday from 1 pm to 8 pm. However, please always double-check the opening hours online should there have been any slight changes in their schedule.

Spandau Citadel.

- **Altstadt Spandau (Spandau Old Town):** Wander through the cobbled streets lined with colorful houses, discover secret courtyards, and relax in quaint cafes. Browse for treasures in antique shops, admire the Gothic Nikolaikirche, and soak in the relaxed atmosphere.

You can visit any time you want.

Altstadt Spandau.
Ingolf from Berlin , Deutschland, CC BY-SA 2.0 <https://creativecommons.org/licenses/by-sa/2.0>, via Wikimedia Commons: https://commons.wikimedia.org/wiki/File:Berlin_-_U-Bahnhof_Altstadt_Spandau_(8479696353).jpg

- **Kolk:** Travel back in time to the heart of Spandau, where half-timbered houses spill medieval secrets and narrow alleys lead to unexpected gems. Explore the St. Nikolai Kirche, climb the Glockenturm for panoramic views, and discover the cozy Kneipen tucked away in this historic corner.

You can visit any time you want.

Kolk.

Ymblanter, CC BY-SA 4.0 <https://creativecommons.org/licenses/by-sa/4.0>, via Wikimedia Commons: https://commons.wikimedia.org/wiki/File:Delft_Kolk_28-30.jpg

- **Spandauer Forst:** Escape the city's hustle and bustle and embrace the tranquility of this vast forest. Hike or bike through shady trails, discover hidden lakes and ponds, and breathe the fresh air. Picnic amid the serene greenery, rent a boat on Havel Lake, and reconnect with nature.

You can visit any time you want.

Spandauer Forst.
Leonhard Lenz, CC BY-SA 4.0 <https://creativecommons.org/licenses/by-sa/4.0>, via Wikimedia Commons: https://commons.wikimedia.org/wiki/File:Path_in_the_Spandauer_Forst_16.jpg

- **Siemensstadt:** Step into a modernist utopia at this UNESCO World Heritage Site. Marvel at the Bauhaus-inspired architecture, the communal gardens, and the innovative urban planning. Explore the Siemensstadt Museum, learn about the history of this pioneering social housing project, and appreciate the vision of the past that shaped the future.

You can visit any time you want.

Siemesstadt.

mibuchat from Siemensstadt, Germany, CC BY-SA 2.0 <https://creativecommons.org/licenses/by-sa/2.0>, via Wikimedia Commons: https://commons.wikimedia.org/wiki/File:Siemensstadt_-_Siemensstadt_(30393913422).jpg

Did You Know: Spandau's history predates Berlin by 40 years, making it the older sibling of the German capital.

Transport

Ditch the car and embrace the freedom of exploring this captivating district on foot, by bike, or by boat.

- **U-Bahn (Underground):** Lines U7 and U9 connect you to Spandau Altstadt and various parts of the district.
- **S-Bahn (Suburban Trains):** Stations like Spandau and Rathaus Spandau provide quick connections to the city center and beyond.
- **Buses:** Numerous bus lines crisscross the district, ensuring easy access to local attractions and neighborhoods.

- **Bikes:** Rental stations abound, making exploring the city and the Spandauer Forst a breeze.
- **Boats:** Take a scenic boat tour on the Havel River for a unique perspective of the district and its waterfront gems.

Did You Know: The Spandau Citadel is one of the best-preserved Renaissance fortresses in Europe.

Experiences

Spandau offers experiences as particular as its character:

- **Time Travel Tour:** Explore Spandau through the ages on a guided tour, visiting key historical sites like the Citadel and Altstadt and uncovering stories of knights, merchants, and revolutionaries.
- **Art and Culture Crawl:** Discover Spandau's beautiful artistic spirit by visiting galleries, studios, and museums. Experience live music in historic churches, enjoy open-air theater in the Citadel courtyard, and cover yourself in the district's creative energy.
- **Festival Fun:** Throughout the year, Spandau comes alive with lively festivals, from the buzzing Christmas markets in Altstadt Spandau to the Spandau Beer Festival, enticing local brews and Bavarian bites against the backdrop of the Citadel. Drown yourself in the festive atmosphere, enjoy live music, and experience the local traditions.
- **Culinary Adventure:** Embark on a delicious journey through Spandau's culinary scene. Savor local specialties like "Spandauer Schrippe" (bread) and "Spandauer Spreewalzen" (fish dumplings) at traditional taverns. Dine in Michelin-starred restaurants with panoramic views at Grunewald, or indulge in international flavors at cafes and bars in modern quarters.

Did You Know: Spandau's Kolk is the oldest part of the district, dating back to the 13th century.

Family Fun

Pack your curiosity, appetite, and your sense of adventure, and prepare to create lasting memories in this beautiful and welcoming district.

- **Spandauer Forst Fun:** Build sandcastles on the shores of Havel Lake, paddle in shallow waters, or rent a family boat for an adventure. Let the kids run wild on the playgrounds in Volkspark Rehberge or explore the interactive exhibits at the Kinder- und

Jugendmuseum (Children's and Youth Museum).

- **Citadel Treasure Hunt:** Tackle a thrilling treasure hunt within the Spandau Citadel walls, following clues and solving puzzles to uncover hidden secrets and stories. This interactive experience promises fun and learning for the whole family.

- **Swimming Fun:** Take a refreshing dip in one of Spandau's many pools, such as the modern Sports and Leisure Center Hakenfelde or the family-friendly Stadtbad Gatow. Enjoy water slides, diving boards, and splash pools for hours of aquatic fun.

- **Siemensstadt Discovery Tour:** Introduce your children to the world of science and technology with a family-friendly tour through Siemensstadt. Learn about inventions, explore interactive exhibits, and test your skills in robotics workshops.

Where to Eat

Spandau tantalizes your taste buds with a diverse culinary scene:

- **Gaststätte G7 (German restaurant):** Enjoy a hearty and authentic German dining experience at Gaststätte G7. This cozy restaurant features a menu of classic dishes like schnitzel and sausages, perfect for a casual lunch or dinner. Be sure to try their homemade apple strudel for dessert.

- **Havel Bistro:** Savor stunning river views while indulging in fresh, seasonal cuisine at Havel Bistro. This modern bistro offers an ever-changing menu that highlights local ingredients, with a focus on seafood dishes.

- **Restaurant Alt-Spandau (Croatian restaurant):** Take a trip to Croatia without leaving Spandau. Restaurant Alt-Spandau serves a delectable array of Croatian specialties, from cevapcici (grilled sausages) to sarma (stuffed vine leaves). The warm atmosphere and friendly service make this a great spot for a memorable meal.

- **Hasir (Turkish restaurant):** Undertake a culinary journey to Turkey at Hasir. This popular restaurant offers a wide range of traditional Turkish dishes, from succulent kebabs to flavorful meze platters. The vibrant atmosphere and attentive staff will make you feel right at home.

- **La Bottega Da Franco (Italian restaurant):** Craving a taste of Italy? La Bottega Da Franco is the perfect solution. This charming restaurant serves up all your favorite Italian classics, from wood-fired pizzas and pasta to fresh salads and decadent desserts.

Did You Know: Siemensstadt, a UNESCO World Heritage Site, is a pioneering example of social housing and urban planning.

Shopping Guide

Whether you're a treasure hunter or a fashion enthusiast, Spandau offers a haven for your shopping desires:

- **Spandau Arcaden:** This modern shopping mall is your one-stop shop for everything from fashion apparel and electronics to homeware stores and grocery options. Enjoy convenient parking, a variety of cafes and restaurants, and even a cinema for a complete shopping and entertainment experience.

- **New Staaken Center:** Explore a more local shopping vibe at the New Staaken Center. This mall features a mix of familiar brand names alongside independent stores, offering a chance to discover unique finds.

- **Bolu Supermarket:** Stock up on groceries, household items, and personal care products at Bolu Supermarket. This supermarket chain offers competitive prices and a wide selection of products, making it a convenient option for grabbing everyday essentials.

Entertainment

Spandau offers a range of entertainment options for those seeking a cultural evening or a cozy night in:

- **Jugendtheaterwerkstatt Spandau e.V.:** Immerse yourself in the world of performing arts at the Jugendtheaterwerkstatt Spandau e.V. This youth theatre company produces a variety of plays and performances throughout the year, offering a chance to experience fresh and innovative productions.

- **Theater Zitadelle:** Journey through time and experience the magic of live theatre at the enchanting Theater Zitadelle. Housed within the historic Spandau Citadel fortress, this unique venue stages a diverse program of plays, concerts, and other cultural events. The open-air courtyard provides a breathtaking backdrop for summer performances.

- **Openairkino Spandau:** Enjoy a classic summer night out at Openairkino Spandau. This outdoor movie theater screens a variety of films throughout the summer months, offering a unique and atmospheric way to enjoy your favorite movies. Pack a picnic basket, grab a blanket, and settle in for a memorable cinematic experience under the starry Spandau sky.

Did You Know: One of Spandau's most famous residents was philosopher and political economist Karl Marx, who briefly lived in the district.

Sports and Leisure

From exploring the vast Spandauer Forst to enjoying water sports on Havel Lake, Spandau provides ample opportunities for an active and healthy lifestyle.

- **Cliffhanger Boulderlounge (Rock climbing gym):** Test your strength and agility at Cliffhanger Boulderlounge. This popular rock climbing gym features a variety of climbing walls with routes for all skill levels. It's a great place to have fun, work out, and maybe even surprise yourself with your climbing prowess.

- **Sport Centrum Siemensstadt (Sports complex):** Enjoy a comprehensive fitness experience at Sport Centrum Siemensstadt. This expansive sports complex offers a wide range of facilities, including swimming pools, indoor courts for tennis, badminton, and squash, a fitness center with state-of-the-art equipment, and group fitness classes. Whether you're looking for a casual swim or an intense workout, Sport Centrum Siemensstadt has something for everyone.

- **Parkour Fitnesspark:** Parkour enthusiasts will rejoice at the Parkour Fitnesspark. This unique outdoor space features a variety of obstacles and challenges designed to test your parkour skills. It's a great place to practice flips, vaults, and precision jumps in a safe and supportive environment.

Accommodations

Pack your bags, choose your spot, and get ready to experience the best of this diverse and captivating district.

- **Select Hotel Berlin Spiegelturm:** For those who appreciate modern style and stunning city views, Select Hotel Berlin Spiegelturm is a perfect choice. This 4-star hotel features bright, comfortable rooms offering a glimpse of the Spandau cityscape. After a day of exploring, unwind at the hotel's sophisticated restaurant or chic bar. The hotel also boasts meeting space, making it a convenient option for business travelers.

- **Centrovital:** Indulge in pure luxury and relaxation at Centrovital. This upscale spa hotel pampers guests with refined rooms and suites, many offering breathtaking lake views. Unwind at the hotel's world-class spa, savor delicious meals at the lake-view restaurant or the bistro/bar, and enjoy the tranquil atmosphere. Centrovital is a perfect choice for travelers seeking a rejuvenating getaway.

- **Ibis Berlin Spandau:** If you're looking for a stylish and affordable option, Ibis Berlin Spandau is a great choice. This laid-back hotel offers contemporary rooms with all the essentials for a comfortable stay. The hotel's funky 24/7 bar provides a lively atmosphere to unwind after a day of exploring. Ibis Berlin Spandau is ideal for budget-conscious travelers who still appreciate a touch of modern design.

Steglitz-Zehlendorf and Spandau are more than just destinations on a map. They are where stories unfold, connections are forged, and memories are made. Whether you stroll through the Kolk, hand in hand with a loved one, or cycle through the Grunewald forest, surrounded by trees, these districts hold the magic of creating moments that linger long after your departure. Let their charms wash over you, allow their history to seep into your soul, and discover the joy of truly experiencing a place, not merely *visiting* it.

Chapter 7: Treptow-Köpenick

Stepping into Treptow-Köpenick is like going through a portal into another Berlin. Gone are the bustling streets and towering blocks. In their place are verdant forests, serene lakes, and tales of forgotten empires. It's the city's most extensive and greenest corner, where centuries-old castles brush shoulders with sprawling parks and sparkling waterways. Here, Berliners find solace in sun-dappled pathways while tourists discover a past etched deeply into palaces and monuments. Whether you're seeking quiet contemplation or energetic exploration, Treptow-Köpenick offers a sanctuary within Berlin, inviting wanderers to discover its secrets hidden beneath the leafy canopy.

Historical Background

Treptow-Köpenick boasts a rich and often turbulent history. First mentioned in 1237, Köpenick was a separate town until 1920. It was renowned for its castle and the infamous "Captain of Köpenick" story of a cobbler posing as a military officer and robbing the town hall. With its industrial heritage, Treptow developed along the Spree, while vast green spaces like Wuhlheide offered recreation. Today, this borough blends its urban past with natural allure, providing a glimpse into Berlin's multifaceted character.

Transport

Treptow-Köpenick offers a variety of options to suit your pace and mood.

- **U-Bahn (Subway) and S-Bahn (Train):** Efficient and widespread, these networks connect you to key attractions and beyond.

- **Buses:** Hop on a bus for a slower, more scenic journey, exploring hidden corners and charming neighborhoods.

- **Boats:** Glide across Müggelsee on a leisurely cruise or rent a kayak for an adventurous paddle.

- **Ferry:** Cross the Dahme River in style, connecting Schloss Köpenick with the mainland.

- **Bikes:** Rent a bike and cycle through the parks, along the river, or on dedicated paths, feeling the wind in your hair and the sun on your skin.

- **Walking:** Lace up your shoes and explore at your own pace, discovering hidden gems and soaking in the atmosphere.

Did You Know: Müggelsee, the largest Berlin lake, was once reserved for Prussian royalty.

Main Attractions

- **Müggelsee and Müggelturm:** Sail across the shimmering expanse of Müggelsee, the largest lake in Berlin, or rent a pedalo for a peaceful adventure. Hike through the surrounding Müggelberge hills and ascend the iconic Müggelturm observation tower for breathtaking panoramic views.

  As of the writing of this book, the normal opening hours are from 10 am to 4 pm from Monday to Friday and 10 am to 5 pm on Saturday and Sunday, but please always double-check the opening hours online should there have been any slight changes in their schedule.

Müggelturm.
Doris Antony, Berlin, CC BY-SA 4.0 <https://creativecommons.org/licenses/by-sa/4.0>, via Wikimedia Commons. https://commons.wikimedia.org/wiki/File:Berlin_Mueggelturm_SE.jpg

- **Altstadt Köpenick:** Wander through the charming cobbled streets of Altstadt Köpenick, dotted with colorful houses, quaint cafes, and the majestic Schloss Köpenick. Admire the Gothic Nikolaikirche, climb the Rathaus Köpenick Tower for city vistas, and soak in the historical ambiance.

  You can visit any time you want.

Altstadt Köpenick.
Rainer Halama, CC BY-SA 4.0 <https://creativecommons.org/licenses/by-sa/4.0>, via Wikimedia Commons. https://commons.wikimedia.org/wiki/File:Berlin-K%C3%B6penick-Altstadt_DSC6887.jpg

- **Schloss Köpenick:** Unearth the opulent past of Prussia at Schloss Köpenick, which now houses the esteemed Kunstgewerbemuseum Berlin. Explore the exquisite decorative art collection, stroll through the landscaped gardens, and imagine the lives of Prussian royals who once graced these halls.

As of the writing of this book, the normal opening hours are from 11 am to 5 pm from Thursday to Sunday, but please always double-check the opening hours online should there have been any slight changes in their schedule.

Schloss Köpenick.

detpurroc, CC BY-SA 3.0 <https://creativecommons.org/licenses/by-sa/3.0>, via Wikimedia Commons. https://commons.wikimedia.org/wiki/File:Schloss_Koepenick_Hofseite.jpg

- **Treptower Park:** De-stress in the vast expanse of Treptower Park, a haven for recreation and reflection. Explore the poignant Soviet War Memorial, wander through the serene gardens, or gaze at the stars at the Archenhold Observatory, home to the world's longest refracting telescope.

  You can visit any time you want.

Treptower Park.

Tim Gage, CC BY-SA 2.0 <https://creativecommons.org/licenses/by-sa/2.0>, via Wikimedia Commons. https://commons.wikimedia.org/wiki/File:Treptower_Park_(7658611018).jpg

- **Spreetunnel:** Embark on an underground adventure by traversing the Spree Tunnel, a pedestrian and bicycle passage connecting Treptower Park with Alt-Treptow. Witness the bustling river life from a new perspective and emerge on the other side to explore gorgeous street art and cafes.

You can visit any time you want.

Spreetunnel.

Pascal Volk, CC BY-SA 2.0 <https://creativecommons.org/licenses/by-sa/2.0>, via Wikimedia Commons. https://commons.wikimedia.org/wiki/File:Spreetunnel_Friedrichshagen.jpg

- **Wuhlheide:** Unleash your inner child at Wuhlheide, a sprawling recreational area teeming with possibilities. Let the kids loose on the playgrounds, bike through scenic trails, or explore the interactive exhibits at the FEZ Berlin, a paradise for family fun.

You can visit any time you want.

Leonhard Lenz, CC0, via Wikimedia Commons.
https://commons.wikimedia.org/wiki/File:Wuhlheide_forest_Berlin_2021-04-20_39.jpg

Experiences

Beyond the must-see sights, Treptow-Köpenick offers a kaleidoscope of experiences that probe its character:

- **Time Travel Tour:** Join a guided tour through Altstadt Köpenick, retracing the footsteps of Prussian kings and the daring "Köpenick Captain." Explore hidden courtyards, discover forgotten stories, and witness history come alive.
- **Art and Culture Crawl:** Find your inner artist in Treptow-Köpenick's remarkable artistic spirit. Visit galleries showcasing local artists, uncover the street art scene in Alt-Treptow, or catch a performance at the Theater am Park.
- **Festival Fun:** Treptow-Köpenick buzzes with lively festivals throughout the year. These events offer a taste of local culture and festive cheer, from the traditional Köpenicker Sommerfest

with its carnival atmosphere to the Christmas markets in Alt-Köpenick.

- **Culinary Adventure:** Embark on a delicious journey through Treptow-Köpenick's diverse culinary scene. Savor fresh seafood at harbor restaurants along the Spree, indulge in authentic Italian cuisine in Alt-Treptow, or try local specialties like "Berliner Boulette" at traditional pubs.

- **Müggelsee Boat Cruise:** Glide across the tranquil waters of Müggelsee on a scenic boat tour. Admire the lush greenery of the surrounding hills, spot water birds, and enjoy the refreshing breeze.

- **Nighttime Kayak Trip:** Paddle under the starry sky on a guided nighttime kayak tour through the canals of Köpenick. Experience the city from a new perspective, listen to the gentle flow of the water, and marvel at the twinkling lights reflected on the surface.

Did You Know: The Archenhold Observatory houses the world's longest refracting telescope, capable of viewing stars 2 billion light-years away.

Family Fun

From historical tours and art crawls to family adventures and culinary delights, Treptow-Köpenick offers experiences to families of all ages:

- **Wuhlheide Adventure:** Build sandcastles on the shores of the Strandbad Wuhlheide, take a family bike ride through the scenic trails, or let the kids loose on the playgrounds. Explore the FEZ Berlin with its interactive exhibits and exciting shows, or enjoy a picnic in the greenery.

- **Müggelsee Water Fun:** Rent a pedalo or kayak and explore the hidden coves of Müggelsee, enjoy a refreshing swim in the lake, or build sandcastles on the shores. The Müggelturm offers panoramic views and a sense of accomplishment for little adventurers.

- **Spreetunnel Treasure Hunt:** Embark on a thrilling treasure hunt with the kids, following clues hidden around the Spreetunnel and Altstadt Köpenick. Discover historical facts, solve riddles, and unearth hidden gems.

- **Spielplatz Köpenick (Playground Köpenick):** This expansive playground in the heart of Köpenick is a paradise for children of all ages. Featuring climbing structures, swings, slides, and a sandpit, it promises hours of laughter and endless fun.

Did You Know: Treptower Park's Soviet War Memorial features a colossal statue of a grieving soldier, commemorating the fallen Red Army soldiers in WWII.

Where to Eat

Treptow-Köpenick tantalizes your taste buds with a diverse culinary scene:

- **Waterfront Dining:** Savor fresh seafood and breathtaking views at harbor restaurants like Fischerei Köpenick or Restaurant Köpenicker Seeterrassen. Enjoy a romantic sunset dinner on the terrace or sip cocktails under the starry sky.
- **Alt-Köpenick Delights:** Explore the charming cobbled streets of Alt-Köpenick and discover hidden gems like Trattoria Alt-Köpenick with its authentic Italian fare or Alt-Treptower Gasthaus for hearty German specialties.
- **Local Markets:** Stock up on fresh produce, artisanal cheeses, and homemade treats at the lively farmers' markets in Alt-Treptow and Rathaus Köpenick. Chat with local vendors, sample local specialties, and soak in the vibrant atmosphere.

Shopping Guide

Shopping in Treptow-Köpenick is a treasure hunt, offering custom-made finds and local charm alongside mainstream options:

- **Alt-Köpenick Boutiques:** Browse through charming boutiques lining the cobbled streets of Alt-Köpenick, discovering handcrafted jewelry, stylish clothing, and quirky souvenirs. Find locally designed homeware at shops like Atelier am Schloss or pick up a piece of Berlin art at Galerie im Alten Rathaus.
- **Wuhlheide Flea Market:** Hunt for bargains and hidden gems at the bustling Wuhlheide Flea Market, held every Sunday. Unearth vintage treasures, antique furniture, collectibles, and everyday essentials in a vibrant atmosphere.
- **Concept Stores:** Discover curated fashion, lifestyle, and design collections at modern concept stores. Explore new brands, find gifts, and let your creative spirit wander.
- **Spreeufer Flohmarkt (Spring Market):** This seasonal market held along the Spreeufer in springtime is a delight for foodies and

design enthusiasts. Sample local delicacies, browse crafts and artwork, and enjoy the lively riverside atmosphere.

- **Shopping Centers:** For everyday needs and mainstream brands, head to shopping centers like Park Center Treptow, with its diverse stores, or the modern Forum Köpenick. Take advantage of convenient Öffnungszeiten (opening hours) and enjoy a relaxed shopping experience.

Did You Know: The pedestrian and bicycle tunnel, Spreetunnel, was secretly built by East Germany and opened shortly before the fall of the Berlin Wall.

Entertainment

While nightlife may not be the main draw of Treptow-Köpenick, it offers a range of entertainment options for those seeking a cultural evening or a cozy night in:

- **CineStar Berlin:** Nestled in Treptower Park, CineStar Berlin showcases independent films, arthouse gems, and cult classics in a cozy and atmospheric setting. Relax on plush sofas, sip on cocktails, and discover independent cinema.
- **Comedy Nights:** Get your giggles at regular stand-up comedy nights in venues like Comedy Café or Laughing Spree. Discover rising stars, witness established comedians, and prepare for an evening of side-splitting laughter.
- **Home Entertainment:** Relax in your cozy accommodation and enjoy a night in with streaming services, board games, or a movie marathon. Many hotels and apartments in Treptow-Köpenick offer comfortable spaces and entertainment options.

Sports and Leisure

Treptow-Köpenick encourages an active lifestyle and outdoor adventures:

- **Müggelsee Water Sports:** Paddleboard, kayak, or sail across the expansive Müggelsee, enjoying the refreshing breeze and stunning scenery. Rent equipment from Müggelsee Bootsverleih or join a guided tour.
- **Hiking and Cycling:** Explore the scenic Müggelberge hills on numerous hiking trails, offering breathtaking views of the lake and surrounding forests. Bike through Treptower Park on dedicated cycling paths, or rent a bike at the Fahrradverleih

Müggelsee for a leisurely ride.

- **Wuhlheide Activities:** Climb on the high ropes course at the FEZ Berlin, conquer the climbing wall at Kletterhalle Wuhlheide, or go bowling at Bowling Spreehöfe. This vibrant area offers endless possibilities for adrenaline rushes and family fun.

- **Winter Fun:** Treptower Park transforms into a wonderland of frozen fun in winter. Glide across the ice rink, sled down snowy hills, or take a horse-drawn carriage ride through the snow-covered landscape.

Did You Know: FEZ Berlin, Europe's largest children's recreation center, boasts interactive exhibits, playgrounds, and workshops, making it a family haven.

Accommodations

Treptow-Köpenick offers a diverse range of accommodations to suit your needs and budget:

- **Historic Hotels:** Experience the charm of a bygone era at Hotel Müggelsee, offering lakefront views and historic ambiance.

- **Modern Apartment:** Modern apartment complexes like Adapt Apartments or Nena Apartments Spreeblau are perfect for families or groups seeking spacious and comfortable accommodations. Relax in fully equipped kitchens, enjoy private balconies, and experience the convenience of apartment living.

- **Ferienwohnungen (Holiday Apartments):** Learn about local life by staying in a Ferienwohnung, offering authentic experiences and comfortable spaces in traditional neighborhoods. Find cozy apartments in Alt-Köpenick with cobblestone streets outside your window or charming lakefront retreats by Müggelsee.

- **Hostels:** Budget-conscious travelers can find affordable and social accommodation at Neohostel Berlin. Meet fellow travelers, enjoy shared spaces like kitchens and lounge areas, and experience the peacefully chaotic atmosphere of hostel life.

- **Guesthouses and Bed & Breakfasts:** Experience personalized hospitality and charming settings at Pension am Schonungsnerg or Müggelseepension, which is perfect for solo travelers or romantic getaways. Enjoy delicious breakfasts, friendly interactions with hosts, and insights into local life.

Treptow-Köpenick transcends the label of mere "borough." It's a microcosm of Berlin, a city within a city. Its cobbled streets hold tales of emperors and revolutionaries, while its leafy trails invite quiet contemplation. Here, the tales of World War II mingle with the laughter of children playing in the shadow of historical landmarks. This blend of the past and present, of urban grit and natural splendor, makes Treptow-Köpenick a destination for sightseeing and experiencing the very essence of Berlin's multifaceted spirit.

Chapter 8: Marzahn-Hellersdorf

Marzahn-Hellersdorf rises from the eastern plains of Berlin, not with grand monuments or bustling avenues but with a canvas of concrete. Remnants of a bygone era, Towering Plattenbauten is a testament to a great vision for housing the masses. Yet, this urban district is surprisingly dynamic. Within the geometric grids of prefabricated blocks, life unfolds in communities, and artistic expression bursts from unexpected corners. Marzahn-Hellersdorf beckons you to peel back the layers, see beyond the surface, and discover the beating heart of a borough in constant transformation.

Historical Background

Marzahn-Hellersdorf, like a patchwork quilt, weaves together threads of history from diverse epochs. Its rural roots stretch back to medieval villages, with Hellersdorf first mentioned in 1375 and Marzahn dating back even further. Quiet farming communities thrived, their lives punctuated by the seasons and the rhythm of the land.

The 20th century ushered in dramatic shifts. The roar of industry echoed through Marzahn with the arrival of factories in the early 1900s, drawing in workers and shaping a new urban identity. However, a dark chapter unfolded during World War II, with Marzahn becoming the site of a forced labor camp for Romani people, a stark reminder of the horrors inflicted under Nazi rule.

The post-war era saw Marzahn reborn as a showcase city of the German Democratic Republic. From the late 1970s onward, vast Plattenbau housing estates rose from the fields, a bold attempt to address the housing shortage. While criticized for their uniformity, these prefabricated blocks housed a vibrant community, nurturing camaraderie and shared history.

Following German reunification, Marzahn-Hellersdorf faced integration and transformation challenges. The borough embraced its heritage, preserving its historical villages and breathing new life into the Plattenbau with colorful murals and innovative projects. Today, it stands as a testament to resilience, where the past and present intertwine, and the future holds the promise of a vibrant, diverse, and ever-evolving community.

Main Attractions

Marzahn-Hellersdorf might surprise you with its abundant green spaces and hidden historical treasures. From international gardens to serene lakes, here are some must-see attractions:

• **Gardens of the World (Gärten der Welt):** Undertake a global journey without leaving the borough. This sprawling park boasts themed gardens from China, Japan, the Orient, and beyond. Stroll through serene bamboo groves, marvel at intricate pagodas, and soak in the vibrant colors of exotic flora. Don't miss the Cable Car in Gärten der Welt, which has breathtaking aerial views of this botanical wonderland.

As of the writing of this book, the normal opening hours are from 9 am to 6 pm from Monday to Sunday, but please always double-check the opening hours online should there have been any slight changes in their schedule.

Gärten der Welt.
https://commons.wikimedia.org/wiki/File:G%C3%A4rten_der_Welt,_Berlin-Marzahn_065.jpg

- **Biesdorf Palace and Palace Gardens:** Step back in time at the elegant Biesdorf Palace, a 19th-century architectural gem. Explore the grand halls adorned with intricate decorations and wander through the landscaped gardens, a haven of manicured lawns and fragrant flowerbeds.

As of the writing of this book, the normal opening hours are from 10 am to 6 pm from Saturday to Monday and Wednesday and Thursday, and 12 pm to 9 pm on Friday, but please always double-check the opening hours online should there have been any slight changes in their schedule.

Biesdorf Palace.

- **Kienbergpark and Kienberg Hill:** This park combines historical landmarks with stunning natural beauty. Discover architectural gems like the Wolkenhain observation tower, the Wuhlesteg suspension bridge, and the Tälchenbrücke, nestled amid the rolling hills and lush greenery of the Kienberg and Wuhletal. Hike to the top of Kienberg Hill for panoramic views that will leave you breathless.

You can visit any time you want.

- **Kaulsdorfer Lakes:** Escape the urban bustle and find peace by the Kaulsdorfer Lakes. These tranquil waters offer stunning scenery, perfect for leisurely walks, bike rides, or simply soaking up the sun. Take a paddleboat across the glassy surface and enjoy the serene atmosphere.

You can visit any time you want.

Kaulsdorfer Lakes.

- **Wuhlgarten (Wuhl Garden):** This vast green space is your gateway to nature. Get lost in a maze of meadows and pathways, breathe in the fresh air, and enjoy the quiet beauty of this urban oasis. Picnic on the lush grass, take a stroll, or explore the hidden trails and ponds.

You can visit any time you want.

Transport

Navigating Marzahn-Hellersdorf offers diverse transportation options at your fingertips. Whether you're a public transport enthusiast, a cycling champion, or a dedicated walker, the borough caters to your preferred pace and style.

Public Transport:

- **S-Bahn and U-Bahn:** The S-Bahn (suburban trains) and U-Bahn (underground) offer the most efficient way to explore beyond the borough. Hop on lines S7, S3, or U5 and connect to major attractions in central Berlin.

- **Buses:** An extensive bus network, including night buses, crisscrosses the borough, providing access to every corner. Lines 154, 255, and 169 are particularly handy for exploring key areas.

- **Trams:** Trams offer a scenic way to get around, especially in Hellersdorf. Line M6 connects the district to other parts of the city.

For the Active Traveler:

- **Cycling:** Marzahn-Hellersdorf is a cyclist's haven with dedicated paths and bike lanes running alongside many major roads. Rent a bike and explore the scenic Kaulsdorfer Lakes or navigate the green expanse of Wuhlgarten.

- **Walking:** Lace up your walking shoes and discover the hidden gems of the borough on foot. Take a stroll through the charming village of Kaulsdorf or conquer Kienberg Hill for panoramic vistas.

Additional Options:

- **Taxis:** Taxis are readily available throughout the borough, offering a convenient option for late-night journeys or luggage-laden travelers.

- **Car-sharing:** Several car-sharing companies operate in the area, providing a flexible and economical option for those who prefer driving.

Note: Tickets for all public transport options can be purchased using the BVG app or directly from ticket machines. Single tickets, day passes, and tourist cards are available, depending on your travel needs.

Did You Know: Gärten der Welt, a sprawling park within Marzahn-Hellersdorf, is a miniature globe of gardens. Explore Japanese tea gardens, stroll through Italian vineyards, and marvel at Chinese pagodas, all within a few steps.

Experiences

Marzahn-Hellersdorf is more than a collection of sights. It's a canvas of experiences waiting to be painted with your footsteps. So, grab your curiosity and delve into the borough with these thematic adventures:

Cultural Medley:

- **Global Gardens Tour:** Embark on a sensory journey through the Gardens of the World. Learn about traditional Chinese tea ceremonies, witness Japanese koi gliding through ponds, and savor the aromas of Middle Eastern spices.
- **History Hunt:** Uncover the borough's hidden stories on a guided walking tour. Explore the charming village of Kaulsdorf, discover the industrial past of Marzahn, or stand on the grounds of the former forced labor camp, a poignant reminder of the past.
- **Art in Unexpected Places:** Keep your eyes peeled for murals adorning buildings. Take a street art tour and discover the stories and messages hidden within the concrete canvases.
- **Theater am Park:** Catch classic plays, contemporary productions, and children's theater in this intimate and vibrant theater. Enjoy post-show discussions, meet the actors, and enchant yourself with the magic of live performance.

Nature's Playground:

- **Paddle Power:** Rent a kayak or canoe and explore the tranquil waters of the Kaulsdorfer Lakes. Glide past lush reed beds, spot sunbathing turtles, and discover hidden coves.
- **Cycling Spree:** Hop on a bike and pedal through the sprawling Wuhlgarten, a haven for nature lovers. Follow scenic paths,

climb the Kienberg Hill for breathtaking views, and picnic in the meadows.

- **Birdwatching Bonanza:** Take a guided birdwatching tour through the Kienbergpark and Wuhletal. Spot colorful woodpeckers, listen to the tuneful songs of warblers, and learn about the diverse birdlife that thrives in the city.

Festival Fun:

- **Karneval der Kulturen:** Witness the energy of the Carnival of Cultures, a kaleidoscope of music, dance, and costumes celebrating diversity and unity.

- **Gärten der Welt Festivals:** Entertain yourself with the many cultural festivities held throughout the year at the Gardens of the World. From Chinese New Year celebrations to Japanese cherry blossom festivals, each event offers a fascinating melded cultural experience.

- **Sommer im Kiez:** Join the locals at the "Summer in the Kiez" festival, a celebration of community spirit with live music, street food stalls, and family-friendly activities.

Did You Know: Step into a perfectly preserved 1970s apartment at the Museumswohnung. From floral wallpaper to vintage appliances, this untouched apartment offers a fascinating glimpse into daily life under the GDR.

Family Fun

Marzahn-Hellersdorf isn't only for grown-ups. It's a playground for imaginations of all sizes, a treasure trove of experiences waiting to be explored with little adventurers in tow. Pack the strollers, grab the sunscreen, and get ready for some serious family fun.

Nature Nests:

- **Gärten der Welt:** Let your little ones embark on a global safari without leaving Berlin. Explore the Chinese Garden's miniature pandas, climb the bamboo maze in the Japanese Garden, and marvel at the colorful koi in the Oriental Garden. Picnic by the waterfall or take a scenic ride on the cable car for unforgettable memories.

- **Kaulsdorfer Lakes:** Pack your swimsuits and sunscreen for a day of family fun by the water. Build sandcastles on the beach, take a paddleboat adventure, or try your hand at mini-golf at the nearby course. The scenic paths around the lakes are perfect for strolls or energetic bike rides.

- **Wuhlgarten:** This sprawling green space is a paradise for little explorers. Let them loose on the giant playgrounds, chase butterflies in the meadows, or follow the exciting nature trails with hidden surprises around every corner. Pack a picnic and enjoy a relaxing afternoon under the trees.

Indoor Escapades:

- **Spielstadt Bambolino:** Rain or shine, this indoor playground is a guaranteed hit. Slides, climbing towers, bouncy castles, and ball pits create a world of laughter and imagination. There's even a separate toddler area for the littlest explorers.

- **Biesdorf Palace:** Step back in time with a visit to this majestic palace. The grand halls, intricate decorations, and sprawling gardens will enchant kids. Take a guided tour, or let them run wild on the manicured lawns.

- **Kulturhaus Hellersdorf:** This cultural center offers a variety of family-friendly activities throughout the year. There's something for every child's interest, from puppet shows and theater performances to workshops and arts and crafts sessions.

Special Events:

- **Sommer im Kiez:** Join the lively "Summer in the Kiez" festival for a day of fun and laughter. Face painting, bouncy castles, street performers, and family-friendly concerts create unforgettable memories.

- **Gärten der Welt Festivals:** Throughout the year, the Gardens of the World host special events with a family-friendly twist. From pumpkin carving in autumn to lantern festivals in winter, there's always something magical to discover.

Did You Know: The Helle Mitte shopping center in Hellersdorf boasts Europe's largest indoor climbing park, perfect for adrenaline junkies. The same complex houses the impressive Ernst Busch Theater, showcasing opera, ballet, and drama performances.

Where to Eat

Marzahn-Hellersdorf is a melting pot of flavors, offering a diverse culinary scene that goes beyond the typical Berlin fare. From traditional German comfort food to international specialties and trendy bistros, your taste buds are in for a treat. Here are some delectable options to whet your appetite:

Local Delights:

- **Landhaus Marzahner Krug:** This traditional German restaurant serves hearty classics like schnitzel, sausages, and potato dumplings in a cozy atmosphere. Don't miss the "Marzahner Teller," a platter showcasing local specialties.

- **La Paz:** Enjoy the authentic Mexican flavors at La Paz. Vibrant cocktails, sizzling fajitas, and authentic mole sauce are a few highlights on the menu, served in a lively, friendly atmosphere.

- **Sakura Garten:** This stylish restaurant offers a fusion of Thai, Chinese, and Japanese cuisine. Fresh sushi, flavorful curries, and delicious dim sum are just a few temptations on the menu.

Global Gastronomy:

- **Call a Pizza:** Craving a classic Italian pizza? Call a Pizza delivers the goods with fresh ingredients and generous toppings. Choose from a variety of traditional pizzas or create your masterpiece.

- **Trattoria La Stalla:** This charming trattoria brings a taste of Italy to Marzahn-Hellersdorf. Enjoy homemade pasta dishes, wood-fired pizzas, and fresh seafood in a rustic setting.

Hidden Gems:

- **Das Kleine Eiswerk:** Beat the heat with a scoop (or two) of homemade ice cream at Das Kleine Eiswerk. Choose from classic flavors like vanilla and chocolate to more adventurous options like mango and pistachio.

- **Restaurant im Kienbergpark:** After exploring Kienbergpark, indulge in a delicious meal at the park's restaurant, Wolke Sieben. Enjoy panoramic views, seasonal dishes, and a relaxed atmosphere.

Bonus Tip: Keep an eye out for local farmers' markets, where you will find fresh produce, regional specialties, and delicious treats. The Marzahn farmers' market takes place every Wednesday and Saturday, offering a vibrant slice of local life.

Did You Know: Marzahn-Hellersdorf has nurtured several Olympic champions, including world-renowned discus thrower Robert Harting and swimmer Franziska van Almsick.

Shopping Guide

Marzahn-Hellersdorf might surprise you with its shopping scene, with something for every budget and style. Whether you're a savvy bargain hunter or a discerning boutique browser, get ready to fill your bags with treasures.

- **EASTGATE Berlin:** Immerse yourself in retail therapy at EASTGATE Berlin. This expansive shopping mall boasts a comprehensive collection of stores featuring everything from fashion apparel and electronics to homeware stores and restaurants. Enjoy convenient parking facilities, a variety of cafes and eateries, and even a cinema for a complete shopping and entertainment experience.

- **Marktplatz Center Hellersdorf:** Experience the local shopping atmosphere at Marktplatz Center Hellersdorf. This neighborhood shopping center features a variety of smaller stores, cafes, and service providers. It's a great place to find everyday essentials, grab a coffee, and support local businesses.

- **SpreeCenter:** For a more traditional department store experience, head to SpreeCenter. This mid-sized department store offers a variety of departments for clothing, shoes, cosmetics, homewares, and more. It's a convenient one-stop shop for a variety of your shopping needs.

Bonus Tip: Don't forget to check out the Christmas markets in Marzahn-Hellersdorf during the festive season. Enjoy the twinkling lights, browse handcrafted ornaments and gifts, and enjoy delicious treats at the food stalls.

Entertainment

Marzahn-Hellersdorf is not only about historical sights and peaceful parks. After a day of exploration, prepare to be entertained. From big-screen thrills to local artistic sparks, this borough packs a punch in the entertainment department.

- **UCI Am Eastgate:** Catch the latest blockbusters and Hollywood premieres in style at UCI Am Eastgate. This modern multiplex cinema features comfortable seating, state-of-the-art projection and sound technology, and a concession stand offering popcorn, drinks, and other movie snacks.
- **Biesdorfer Parkbühne:** During the summer months, the Biesdorfer Parkbühne comes alive with open-air theater productions. This unique venue, situated in a beautiful park setting, offers a delightful way to enjoy a variety of performances, from classic plays to contemporary works. Pack a picnic basket, spread out a blanket under the stars, and immerse yourself in the magic of live theater under the open sky.
- **Theater am Park:** For a more traditional theater experience, head to Theater am Park. This local theater company stages a diverse program of productions throughout the year, including comedies, dramas, and musicals. It's a great opportunity to experience the local theater scene and support the performing arts community.

Bonus Tip: Check out the local events calendar for pop-up festivals, street performances, and live music sessions in parks and public squares. Join in the spontaneous artistic energy and discover hidden talents throughout the borough.

Sports and Leisure

Marzahn-Hellersdorf is a hive for the active soul and the leisurely spirit. Whether you're a fitness fanatic or a sun seeker, this borough has a kaleidoscope of ways to move your body and nourish your mind.

- **Schwimmhalle Helene-Weigel-Platz "Helmut Behrendt":** Take a refreshing dip or train for your next triathlon at Schwimmhalle Helene-Weigel-Platz "Helmut Behrendt." This public indoor swimming pool features a 25-meter lap pool, a separate leisure pool, and a children's pool, making it a great option for swimmers of all ages and abilities. During the summer months, check the opening hours as some pools implement seasonal closures.
- **Beach Volleyball Platz:** Calling all beach volleyball enthusiasts. Head to Beach Volleyball Platz for a friendly game or to practice your skills. This outdoor court provides a fun and social setting in

which to enjoy some exercise and friendly competition in the sunshine.

- **ELIXIA VitalClub GmbH & Co. KG Hellersdorf:** For a more comprehensive fitness experience, ELIXIA VitalClub offers a variety of options. This spa and health club features a state-of-the-art gym with cardio and weight training equipment, group fitness classes, and a relaxing spa area. Whether you're looking to build muscle, improve your cardiovascular health, or simply unwind after a long day, ELIXIA VitalClub has something for you.

Bonus Tip: Check out the diverse sports clubs and organizations in Marzahn-Hellersdorf. From martial arts to dance classes, there's something for everyone to join, learn new skills, and make new friends.

Did You Know: While the prefabricated buildings are iconic, Marzahn-Hellersdorf boasts hidden architectural gems. Discover the charming village of Kaulsdorf with its traditional half-timbered houses, or explore the elegant Schloss Biesdorf, a grand 18th-century palace nestled amid the greenery.

Accommodations

Exploring Marzahn-Hellersdorf requires a comfortable and convenient basecamp. Whether you're a budget-conscious adventurer, a family seeking space, or a luxury seeker, this borough offers a range of accommodation options to suit your needs and desires.

- **Hotel Helle Mitte:** This simple and functional hotel is a great choice for budget-conscious travelers. Hotel Helle Mitte offers clean and comfortable rooms with basic amenities, making it a convenient option for those who prioritize affordability and a good night's sleep. On-site parking and Wi-Fi might be available, so check during booking.

- **Parkhotel Marzahn:** For a more personalized stay, consider Parkhotel Marzahn. This family-run hotel offers a warm and welcoming atmosphere with comfortable rooms and friendly service. Some rooms might even boast balconies overlooking green spaces. The hotel's location near parks might be ideal for those seeking a quieter stay.

- **Gasthof Zum Oberfeld:** Immerse yourself in local history at Gasthof Zum Oberfeld. This traditional guesthouse, established in the 19th century, offers a unique and charming accommodation experience. The guesthouse might feature historical touches and a cozy atmosphere, perfect for those seeking a more characterful stay.

Bonus Tip: Consider eco-friendly accommodations like bed and breakfasts or vacation rentals run by locals. They offer a sustainable experience and support the local community.

Step away from the monolithic facades, and Marzahn-Hellersdorf reveals its hidden depth. Verdant havens like the Gärten der Welt, bursting with exotic flora, transport you to distant shores. Historical gems like Schloss Biesdorf echo tales of aristocratic pasts. In Marzahn-Hellersdorf, the story goes beyond the Plattenbau. It's about people, resilience, and the quiet defiance of urban renewal. It's an invitation to embrace the unexpected, to find beauty in the ordinary, and to witness a borough redefining its narrative.

Chapter 9: Pankow – Reinickendorf

Berlin unfolds in captivating contrasts, and nowhere is this more evident than in the neighboring districts of Pankow and Reinickendorf. Pankow pulses with a bohemian rhythm, its streets alive with art galleries, trendy cafes, and avant-garde theaters. Here, history is evident in grand Wilhelmine villas and cobblestone streets, while modern creativity bursts forth in murals and innovative design studios.

Across the Pankow Canal, Reinickendorf offers a serene counterpoint. Lush forests embrace sparkling lakes, inviting long walks and lazy picnics. History buffs will find treasures in the Prussian palaces and Cold War relics, while families delight in the charming villages and bustling water sports scenes. Get ready to discover the distinct personalities of these two districts, where contrasting landscapes and captivating stories come together to paint a picture of Berlin's multifaceted charm.

Pankow: Berlin's Bohemian Heart

Pankow, a district in northeastern Berlin, is a medley of rich history, artistic spirit, and verdant havens. Its streets hum with the stories of Prussian royalty, bohemian revolutionaries, and contemporary creatives, each layer adding depth to its captivating narrative. Whether you seek artistic inspiration, historical insights, or tranquil escapes, Pankow promises an unforgettable journey.

Historical Background

Once a collection of sleepy villages nestled in rural farmland, Pankow's destiny changed when Frederick the Great's wife, Queen Elisabeth Christine, bestowed upon it the regal elegance of Schönhausen Palace. Prussian summers bloomed with opulent fêtes and strolling courtiers. Their laughter echoed through the manicured gardens. Yet, beneath the veneer of aristocratic splendor, Pankow harbored a growing industrial heart. The 19th century saw factories and tenements rise, transforming the district into a working-class hub buzzing with activity.

Main Attractions

- **Prenzlauer Berg:** Dive into the resonant heart of Pankow, where vintage treasures gleam in Mauerpark's Sunday flea market, cafes spill onto sun-drenched squares, and street art murals tell stories on every corner. Explore Kollwitzplatz, a bustling hub pulsating with life and history, or discover the artistic haven of Kulturbrauerei, a former brewery complex transformed into a cultural center housing galleries, theaters, and cinemas.

You can visit any time you want.

- **Schönhausen Palace:** Step back in time at this elegant palace, its gardens recounting tales of royal summers. Admire the Baroque architecture, stroll through the manicured lawns, and discover the fascinating history of Prussian royalty, who once called this opulent residence their home.

As of the writing of this book, the normal opening hours are from 10 am to 4 pm on Saturday and Sunday, but please always double-check the opening hours online should there have been any slight changes in their schedule.

Schönhausen Palace.
A.Savin, CC BY-SA 3.0 <https://creativecommons.org/licenses/by-sa/3.0>, via Wikimedia Commons. https://commons.wikimedia.org/wiki/File:Berlin_Schloss_Schoenhausen_06-2014.jpg

- **Berlin-Weißensee Cemetery:** Embark on a contemplative journey through this historical cemetery, one of Europe's most extensive Jewish burial grounds. Take in the impressive tombstones and memorials, learn about the rich history of the Jewish community, and visit the New Synagogue, a magnificent landmark that's a testament to faith and resilience.

As of the writing of this book, the normal opening hours are from 7:30 am to 4 pm on Monday and Thursday, from 8 am to 2:30 on Friday, and 8 am to 4 pm on Sunday, but please always double-check the opening hours online should there have been any slight changes in their schedule.

Berlin-Weißensee Cemetery.

- **Wasserturm Prenzlauer Berg:** Ascend this iconic water tower for breathtaking panoramic views of Pankow. Explore the museum housed within, learn about its transformation from industrial marvel to beloved landmark, and soak up the panoramic vistas from the observation deck.

You can visit any time you want.

Wasserturm Prenzlauer Berg.

- **Pankow Town Hall (Rathaus Pankow):** Admire the architectural beauty of this neo-Gothic town hall, a symbol of local governance. Attend events and exhibitions held within, or bask in the charm of the surrounding square with its inviting cafes and shops.

As of the writing of this book, the normal opening hours are from 9:30 am to 8 pm on Monday, Tuesday, Thursday, and Saturday, and from 9:30 am to 1 pm on Friday, but please always double-check the opening hours online should there have been any slight changes in their schedule.

Pankow Town Hall.

- **Botanischer Volkspark Pankow:** Find serenity amid nature's embrace. Explore the themed gardens, from the Alpine Garden's rocky slopes to the Rhododendron Valley's vibrant blooms, and discover rare plants in the greenhouses. Hike along tranquil paths, relax in the shade of towering trees, and indulge in the beauty of this urban oasis.

  Opening hours may differ, so check their website: https://gruen-berlin.de/pressemitteilung/gruen-berlin-gibt-verantwortung-fuer-den-botanischen-volkspark-blankenfelde-pankow-ab

Botanischer Volkspark Pankow.
Fridolin freudenfett, CC BY-SA 4.0 <https://creativecommons.org/licenses/by-sa/4.0>, via Wikimedia Commons.
https://commons.wikimedia.org/wiki/File:Botanischer_Volkspark_Blankenfelde-Pankow-002.jpg

- **Zeiss-Großplanetarium:** Be captivated by the mysteries of the cosmos. Watch immersive shows projected onto the world's largest planetarium dome, explore interactive exhibits that spark curiosity, and embark on a journey through galaxies and star-studded skies, returning with a newfound appreciation for the vastness of the universe.

As of the writing of this book, the normal opening hours are from 9 am to 2 pm from Tuesday to Thursday, 9 am to 12: 30 pm, 3 pm to 8 pm on Friday, and10:30 am to 10 pm on Saturday, and 10 am to 8 pm on Sunday, but please always double-check the opening hours online should there have been any slight changes in their schedule.

Zeiss-Großplanetarium.

Jochen Teufel, CC BY-SA 3.0 <https://creativecommons.org/licenses/by-sa/3.0>, via Wikimedia Commons. https://commons.wikimedia.org/wiki/File:Zeiss-Gro%C3%9Fplanetarium_Berlin_(2009).jpg

Transport

Whether you prefer the speed of the U-Bahn, the charm of a vintage tram, or the freedom of cycling, Pankow's transport options ensure you can effortlessly navigate its vibrant streets and hidden gems. Use the efficient U-Bahn (underground) lines U2 and U8, which connect you to key locations like Pankow Station, Senefelderplatz, and Eberswalder Straße. Trams offer a scenic way to explore specific neighborhoods, with line M13 traversing Prenzlauer Berg and line M2 running through

Weißensee. Buses provide comprehensive coverage, and cycling is a delightful option for short distances, thanks to Pankow's extensive network of dedicated bike lanes.

Main U-Bahn Stations:

- **Pankow Station:** Gateway to the district, connecting you to lines U2 and U8.

- **Senefelderplatz:** Heart of Prenzlauer Berg, offering access to cafes, shops, and cultural attractions.

- **Eberswalder Straße:** Bustling hub with connections to Mauerpark and Kollwitzplatz.

Cycling Tips:

- Rent a bike from numerous cafes and shops or use Berlin's bike-sharing program.

- Explore dedicated bike lanes on Mauerparkstraße, Kollwitzstraße, and Entlang der Panke.

- Helmets are recommended, and traffic regulations apply.

Did You Know: Pankow boasts one of Berlin's highest concentrations of green spaces, offering a welcome escape from the urban bustle.

Experiences

Pankow offers a plethora of sightseeing options. Make contact with the district's spirit through these thematic experiences:

- **Bohemian Wanderings:** Join a walking tour led by local artists to discover the hidden alleyways and courtyards where street art thrives. Learn about the history of the graffiti scene, find hidden murals, and witness the vibrant pulse of Prenzlauer Berg's artistic soul.

- **Culinary Delights:** Embark on a food tour through Pankow's diverse culinary landscape. Sample local specialties at traditional pubs, savor international flavors at trendy cafes, and discover hidden gems tucked away in side streets. Pankow's culinary scene promises a tantalizing adventure for your taste buds, from hearty German fare to innovative fusion cuisine.

- **Historical Recaps:** Bike through Pankow's past, tracing the footsteps of revolutionaries and royalty. Explore the industrial heritage of Wedding, discover the hidden stories of the GDR era, and visit memorials that display moments of resistance and resilience. This cycling tour offers a new perspective on Pankow's multifaceted history.

- **Green Escapes:** Escape the urban buzz and embrace the tranquility of Pankow's green spaces. Join a guided nature walk through the idyllic Botanical Garden, learn about the local flora and fauna, and discover hidden paths leading to unexpected serenity pockets. Alternatively, rent a boat and explore the tranquil waters of the Pankow Canal, enjoying the scenic beauty and fresh air.

Did You Know: The iconic Wasserturm, a symbol of Prenzlauer Berg, has a fascinating history, transforming from a brewery to a fire station before becoming a beloved landmark.

Family Fun

Pankow caters to families with many activities and attractions:

- **Mauerpark Adventures:** Let loose at Mauerpark, a haven for family fun. Kids can climb the iconic amphitheater, explore the playground, and splash in the water fountain. Join the lively flea market on Sundays, hunt for treasures, and enjoy street performances.
- **Zeiss-Großplanetarium Wonders:** Take your family on a journey through the cosmos. Watch educational shows about the planets and stars, marvel at the awe-inspiring visuals projected onto the giant dome, and spark your children's curiosity about the universe.
- **Botanical Garden Exploration:** Embark on a family adventure through the diverse gardens of the Botanischer Volkspark. Let your children run through the Alpine Garden's rocky paths, discover hidden creatures in the ponds, and learn about different plant species in the greenhouses. Pack a picnic and enjoy a relaxing afternoon surrounded by nature.
- **Playgrounds and Parks:** Pankow boasts a plethora of playgrounds and parks perfect for families. Head to Kollwitzplatz for its iconic playground, and let your children run free, enjoy the fresh air, and create lasting memories.

Did You Know: Kollwitzplatz, the heart of Prenzlauer Berg, was named after Rosa Luxemburg, a revolutionary socialist whose spirit continues to resonate through the neighborhood.

Where to Eat

Pankow's culinary scene caters to every palate and budget:

- **International Flavors:** Embark on a global culinary adventure at Dicke Wirtin, a trendy restaurant serving delicious Italian cuisine. Savor pizzas, plates of pasta, and fresh seafood in a vibrant atmosphere.
- **Hidden Gems:** Discover culinary gems tucked away in side streets. For contemporary Vietnamese cuisine, head to Le Minh, while Hanoi Com Viet offers authentic street food delights.

Shopping Guide

Pankow offers a unique shopping experience, blending vintage treasures with contemporary finds:

- **Flea Market Frenzy:** Hunt for bargains at Mauerpark's Sunday flea market, a treasure trove of vintage clothing, furniture, and trinkets. Hone your bargaining skills, discover hidden gems, and soak up the lively atmosphere.
- **Independent Boutiques:** Explore the charming streets of Prenzlauer Berg and discover independent boutiques showcasing local designers and handcrafted goods. From quirky jewelry stores to vintage clothing shops, you'll find pieces to add a touch of Berlin to your wardrobe.
- **Art and Design Havens:** Browse the galleries and design shops lining Kollwitzplatz. Discover contemporary art, handmade ceramics, and homeware imbued with Pankow's creative spirit.
- **Local Markets:** Soak up the local atmosphere at the Arkonaplatz and Kollwitzplatz markets. Pick up fresh produce, flowers, and artisanal treats, and experience the friendly banter of Berliners.

Entertainment

- **Kulturbrauerei:** This former brewery complex is a vibrant hub for live music, theatre, and comedy. Catch up-and-coming bands in the Kesselhaus, watch experimental performances in the Maschinenhalle, or laugh the night away at the Prater Garten open-air stage.
- **Zeiss-Großplanetarium:** Join immersive film experiences beyond the usual. Watch documentary films projected onto the world's largest planetarium dome, embark on virtual reality journeys, and be transported to other worlds through the magic of moving

images.

Bonus Tip: Check out the Pankow events calendar for pop-up festivals, street performances, and special events happening throughout the year. Whether seeking live music in a hidden courtyard or an off-the-wall artistic experience, Pankow always has something to offer.

Did You Know: Berlin-Weißensee Cemetery is the final resting place of many notable figures, including composer Giacomo Meyerbeer and artist Käthe Kollwitz. Their stories are etched into the stones that mark their eternal slumber.

Sports and Leisure

Pankow offers a variety of ways to stay active and unwind:

- **Cycling Tours:** Explore the district on two wheels. Join a guided bike tour through Pankow's historical sites and green spaces, or rent a bike and pedal along the scenic Pankow Canal.

- **Swimming and Boating:** Take a dip in the Badeschiff, a former barge transformed into a floating pool anchored in the Spree River. Alternatively, rent a boat and explore the waterways, enjoying the tranquility and city views from a different perspective.

- **Yoga and Fitness:** Find your inner zen at one of Pankow's many yoga studios and fitness centers. There's something for every fitness level and interest, from yoga in the park to dance classes and TRX workouts.

Did You Know: Zeiss-Großplanetarium holds the Guinness World Record for the largest projector dome in the world, promising a truly immersive journey into the cosmos.

Accommodations

Pankow caters to diverse budgets and preferences:

- **Boutique Hotels:** Experience the bohemian charm of hotels like Myer's Hotel or Linnen. Enjoy stylish rooms, trendy rooftop bars, and a location within the heart of the action.

- **Cozy Apartment Rentals:** Opt for an authentic experience by renting a charming apartment in a traditional Berlin building. Feel like a local, explore side streets, and enjoy the convenience of having your own space.

- **Budget-Friendly Hostels:** Alcatraz Backpacker Hostel offers affordable dorm beds and private rooms for backpackers and solo travelers. Meet fellow travelers, participate in organized activities, and enjoy the hostel's atmosphere.

Pankow's lively spirit, historical charm, and diverse offerings make it a must-visit on a trip to Berlin. Whether you're a seasoned traveler or a first-time visitor, book your stay, lace up your walking shoes, and prepare to be captivated by the bohemian heart of Berlin.

Reinickendorf: Berlin's Green Oasis

Beyond the bustling heart of Berlin lies Reinickendorf, a haven of serene lakes, verdant forests, and charming historical villages. This district, nestled in the city's northwest corner, offers a welcome respite from the urban clamor, inviting you to breathe deeply, reconnect with nature, and discover its hidden treasures.

Historical Background

Reinickendorf's story is a tale of rural serenity and urban expansion. It remained a patchwork of sleepy villages for centuries, with Tegel emerging as its cultural and economic hub. The 19th century witnessed the arrival of industry, transforming Reinickendorf into a center for brickmaking and machine production. Yet, the district clung to its green heart, boasting vast forests and sparkling lakes that became popular recreational destinations for Berliners. Following World War II, Reinickendorf embraced ambitious urban planning projects, giving rise to the modernist Märkisches Viertel and the UNESCO-listed Weisse Stadt, adding a contemporary layer to its history.

Main Attractions

- **Tegeler See:** Sail across the glistening waters, rent a paddleboat for a leisurely exploration, or stroll along the Greenwich Promenade, savoring the tranquility and stunning lake views.

  You can visit any time you want.

Tegeler See.

- **Alt-Tegel:** Wander through the charming streets, admire the traditional architecture, and soak up the atmosphere at the bustling market square. Explore the historic St. Mary's Church, uncover the fascinating history of Tegel Palace, and browse the Humboldt Library's collection of rare books.

You can visit any time you want.

Alt-Tegel.

Fridolin freudenfett, CC BY-SA 4.0 <https://creativecommons.org/licenses/by-sa/4.0>, via Wikimedia Commons. https://commons.wikimedia.org/wiki/File:Tegel_Alt-Tegel-001.JPG

- **Tegeler Fliess:** Let your stress disappear in the serene beauty of the nature reserve. Hike through the wetlands, spot diverse birdlife, and unwind in the meadows, surrounded by the sounds of nature.

You can visit any time you want.

Tegeler Fliess.

- **Tegeler Forst:** Breathe in the crisp air and explore the wooded trails. Cycle through the forest paths, enjoy a picnic under the canopy or find a quiet spot to reconnect with nature's tranquility. You can visit any time you want.

Tegeler Forst.

Graccem, CC BY-SA 4.0 <https://creativecommons.org/licenses/by-sa/4.0>, via Wikimedia Commons.
https://commons.wikimedia.org/wiki/File:Tegeler_Forst_(n%C3%B6rdlicher_Teil)_LSG-02a.jpg

- **Märkisches Viertel:** Discover the district's urban planning masterpiece. Explore the stylish modernist architecture, admire the green spaces, and experience the community spirit of this expansive housing development.

You can visit any time you want.

Märkisches Viertel.
Jörg Blobelt, CC BY-SA 4.0 <https://creativecommons.org/licenses/by-sa/4.0>, via Wikimedia Commons. https://commons.wikimedia.org/wiki/File:20120407020DR_Berlin-Reinickendorf_M%C3%A4rkisches_Viertel.jpg

- **Weisse Stadt:** Be captivated by the sleek lines and white-plastered facades of this UNESCO World Heritage Site. Learn about the Bauhaus movement's influence, admire the architectural details, and appreciate the harmonious blend of modernity and nature.

  You can visit any time you want.

Weisse Stadt.

Did You Know: Reinickendorf is home to Berlin's second-largest lake, Tegeler See, a haven for water sports enthusiasts and nature lovers.

Transport

Getting around Reinickendorf is easy and convenient:

- **U-Bahn:** Lines U6 and U7 directly connect to the city center and other districts.
- **S-Bahn:** Lines S1 and S26 stop at Tegel and Borsigwalde stations, providing access to other parts of Berlin.
- **Buses:** Numerous bus lines connect Reinickendorf's various neighborhoods and attractions.
- **Cycling:** Extensive bike paths make exploring the district on two wheels a breeze.
- **Boats:** Take a scenic boat trip on the Tegeler See for a unique perspective of the district.

Experiences

Reinickendorf offers more than just sightseeing. Explore these thematic experiences:

- **Nature Adventures:** Join a guided hike through the Tegeler Forst, learn about the local flora and fauna, and discover hidden trails and viewpoints. Alternatively, rent a kayak and explore the hidden waterways of the Tegeler See.

- **Architectural Gems:** Embark on a walking tour of Alt-Tegel and the Weisse Stadt. Learn about the history of these districts, marvel at the architectural styles, and discover hidden stories behind the facades.

- **Family Fun:** Take the kids on a boat trip around the Tegeler See, complete with pirate stories and treasure hunts, or explore the playgrounds in the Märkisches Viertel.

- **Cultural Delights:** Attend a concert or performance at the Fontane-Haus or browse the exhibitions at the Heimatmuseum Reinickendorf.

Did You Know: The district boasts one of the largest housing developments in Berlin, the Märkisches Viertel, with its modernist architecture.

Family Fun

Reinickendorf's blend of nature, history, and modern spaces makes it a fantastic destination for families seeking adventure and laughter. Here are some highlights to create lasting memories:

- **Tegeler See Playground Paradise:** Unleash your little ones' energy at the expansive playground near Greenwich Promenade. Featuring wooden climbing structures, swings, slides, and sandpits, it offers hours of fun for all ages. Pack a picnic and enjoy stunning lake views while the kids play.

- **Tegeler Fliess Discovery Tour:** Embark on a family-friendly nature walk through the Tegeler Fliess. Spot birds in the reeds, follow winding paths through meadows, and learn about the diverse ecosystem through interactive exhibits at the nature information center.

- **Märkisches Viertel Treasure Hunt:** Turn the district into a giant playground with a fun treasure hunt. Follow clues hidden around sculptures and squares, solve riddles related to the architecture, and reward yourselves with ice cream.

Where to Eat

Reinickendorf has numerous dining options catering to all palates and budgets:

- **Lakeside Delights:** Savor fresh seafood and panoramic lake views at Fisch- Tegel, a traditional restaurant nestled on the shores of the Tegeler See. Alternatively, grab a casual bite at one of the waterfront cafes along the Greenwich Promenade.

- **Family-Friendly Fare:** Enjoy hearty German classics and kid-friendly menus at Alt-Tegeler Dorfkrug, a cozy restaurant in the heart of Alt-Tegel. Don't miss the delicious schnitzel and homemade apple strudel.

- **International Flavors:** Embark on a culinary adventure in the Märkisches Viertel. Sample Italian pizzas and pasta, indulge in Moroccan tagines, or savor Vietnamese spring rolls in a vibrant atmosphere.

- **Budget-Friendly Bites:** Grab a quick lunch or delicious pastries at one of the local bakeries scattered throughout the district. Alternatively, pack a picnic basket with fresh produce from the Tegel market and enjoy your meal surrounded by the serene beauty of the Tegeler Forst.

- **Sweet Treats:** Satisfy your sweet tooth with ice cream sundaes from Der Eisbär in Alt-Tegel, or indulge in homemade cakes and pastries at the charming cafés in the Weisse Stadt.

Did You Know: Reinickendorf is a haven for wildlife, with over 200 bird species in its forests and wetlands.

Shopping Guide

While Reinickendorf isn't a major shopping destination, it has its own flavor of local treasures:

- **Märkisches Viertel Market:** Browse traditional stalls selling fresh produce, handcrafted goods, and everyday essentials at this bustling market. Soak up the local atmosphere and pick up souvenirs with a nostalgic touch.

- **Weisse Stadt Design:** Discover hidden gems at the small galleries and antique shops within the Weisse Stadt estate. Find vintage furniture, handcrafted jewelry, and homeware inspired by the Bauhaus aesthetic.

- **Alt-Tegel Boutiques:** Explore the charming streets of Alt-Tegel and stumble upon quaint boutiques and artisan shops. Pick up handmade souvenirs, locally crafted ceramics, and artwork reflecting the district's historical charm.
- **Green Thumb's Paradise:** The Garten-Center Tegel is a paradise for plant lovers. Find everything from indoor houseplants to seasonal blooms and gardening supplies while soaking up the atmosphere of this lush garden center.
- **Family-Friendly Fun:** Take the kids on a toy hunt at one of the local toy stores in Reinickendorf. Find board games, educational toys, and outdoor playthings to keep them entertained long after your trip.

Did You Know: The historic village of Alt-Tegel still retains its charm, with cobbled streets, traditional houses, and a remarkable market square.

Sports and Leisure

Reinickendorf caters to active families and those seeking an escape from the urban buzz:

- **Cycling Adventures:** Explore the district and beyond on dedicated bicycle paths. Rent bikes and pedal along the shores of the Tegeler See, cycle through the scenic Tegeler Forst, or join a guided cycling tour for a deeper appreciation of the local landscapes.
- **Water Activities:** Go beyond sightseeing on the Tegeler See. Rent paddleboards, kayaks, or sailboats for a fun day on the water. Take swimming lessons with the whole family or enroll in sailing courses for a new skill to take home.
- **Horseback Riding:** Experience the thrill of horseback riding at one of the many stables in the district. Take lessons for beginners, explore the surrounding countryside on horseback, or enjoy a peaceful pony ride with the kids.
- **Winter Wonderland:** The Tegeler Forst transforms into a magical winter wonderland during the winter months. Go ice skating on the frozen lake, build snowmen in the meadows, or rent cross-country skis for a serene exploration through the snow-covered landscape.
- **Fitness and Wellness:** Stay active and rejuvenate at one of Reinickendorf's many fitness centers and spas. Enjoy swimming

pools, saunas, and various fitness classes, or indulge in relaxing massages and pampering treatments.

Did You Know: The Weisse Stadt is one of the six Berlin Modernism estates inscribed as UNESCO World Heritage Sites, showcasing the architectural legacy of the Bauhaus movement.

Accommodations

Reinickendorf offers diverse accommodation options to suit every budget and preference:

- **Lakeside Retreats:** Wake up to breathtaking lake views at one of the hotels or guesthouses lining the shores of the Tegeler See. Enjoy the tranquility of the location, indulge in water activities right outside your doorstep, and savor delicious lakefront dining.

- **Charming Apartments:** Drench yourself in the local atmosphere by renting an apartment in Alt-Tegel or the Weisse Stadt. Experience the convenience of having your own space, explore the neighborhood like a local, and enjoy the architectural charm.

- **Family-Friendly Hotels:** Find spacious rooms and kid-friendly amenities at hotels like the Hotel Tegel or the Parkhotel Tegel. Playgrounds, swimming pools, and proximity to parks make these hotels ideal for a comfortable and fun family stay.

- **Budget-Conscious Options:** Opt for hostels or guesthouses in the Märkisches Viertel for affordable accommodation. Meet fellow travelers, share experiences, and enjoy the lively atmosphere of this lovely district.

As you leave the final page, Pankow and Reinickendorf will linger in your memory, their distinct melodies intertwining and forming a harmonious chord. Perhaps you'll be captivated by Pankow's pulse, forever chasing the avant-garde art and bohemian charm. Maybe the tranquil shores of Reinickendorf, where history speaks of wisdom and nature offers quiet reflection, will hold your heart. Whatever your journey in these two districts, they leave an indelible mark that Berlin's magic lies not only in its grand avenues but also in the quiet corners where hidden treasures spill their stories.

Chapter 10: City Itineraries and Programs

Berlin is a city where the spirit of reinvention dances in the air. Here's a curated selection of itineraries and programs tailored to diverse interests and traveler types to help you navigate this metropolis. Berlin has something for you whether you're a solo adventurer seeking hidden gems, a history buff chasing the past, or a family on a whirlwind exploration.

Berlin is a city where the spirit of reinvention dances in the air.
https://www.pexels.com/photo/tv-tower-in-berlin-109630/

For the History Buff: 5-Day Historical and Cultural Dive

- **Day 1:** Lose yourself in Berlin's iconic landmarks. Start your day at the Brandenburg Gate, symbolizing unity and resilience. Stroll through Pariser Platz, admiring the neoclassical Akademie der Künste. Learn about German political history with a guided tour of the Reichstag Building, follow it with a visit to the poignant Holocaust Memorial. End your day at the Französische Kirche.

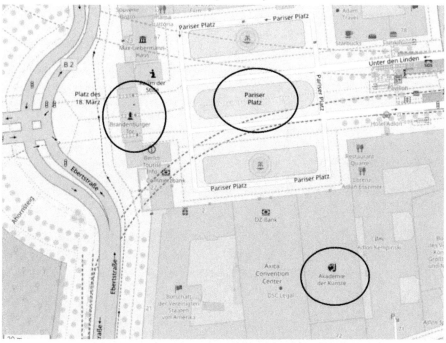

Brandenburger Gate, Pariser Platz and Akademie der Kunste.
OpenStreetMap Contributors https://www.openstreetmap.org

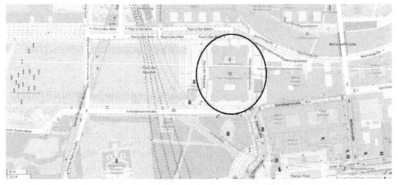

Reichstag Building off Scheidemannstrasse, next to Platz der Republik
OpenStreetMap Contributors https://www.openstreetmap.org

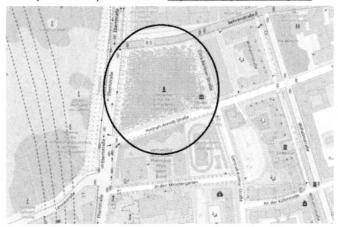

Holocaust Memorial off Ebertstrasse and Behrenstrasse
OpenStreetMap Contributors https://www.openstreetmap.org

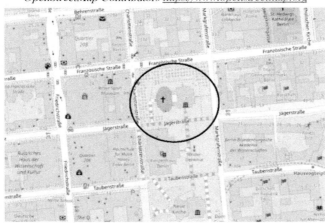

Französische Kirche off Jaegerstrasse and Charlottenstrasse
OpenStreetMap Contributors https://www.openstreetmap.org

- **Day 2:** Explore Museum Island, a UNESCO World Heritage Site boasting five museums. Dive into ancient wonders at the Pergamon Museum, marvel at Egyptian artifacts in the Neues Museum, and discover the city's rich history at the Bode Museum.

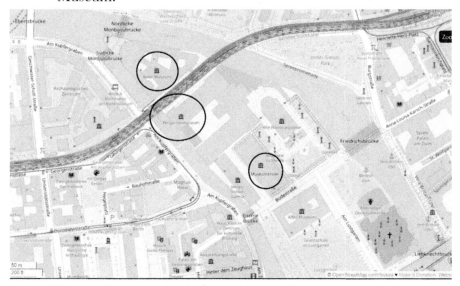

Museum Island

OpenStreetMap Contributors https://www.openstreetmap.org

- **Day 3:** Travel back in time at the Cold War Museum and Checkpoint Charlie, a former border crossing point. Trace the remnants of the Berlin Wall at the East Side Gallery, where artists have transformed its canvas into a powerful open-air exhibition.

Cold War Museum off Unter den Linden
OpenStreetMap Contributors https://www.openstreetmap.org

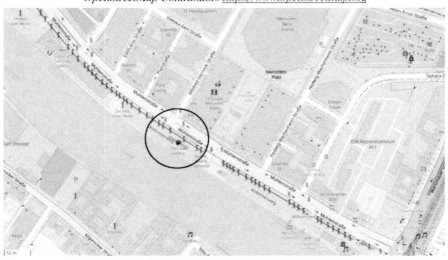

East Side Gallery off Muhlenstrasse
OpenStreetMap Contributors https://www.openstreetmap.org

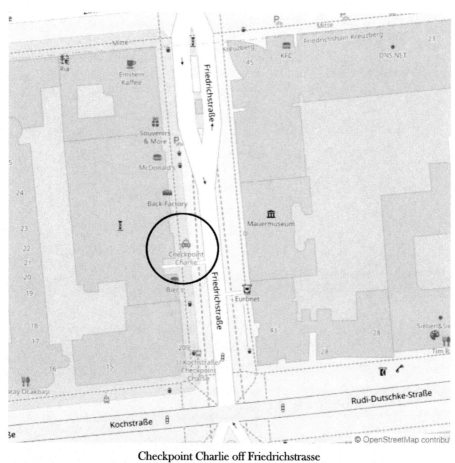

Checkpoint Charlie off Friedrichstrasse

OpenStreetMap Contributors https://www.openstreetmap.org

- **Day 4:** Step into the world of espionage at the fascinating DDR Museum, showcasing the everyday life of East Germany. Explore the Soviet War Memorial in Tiergarten, a poignant reminder of WWII.

DDR Museum off Karl-Liebknecht Strasse
OpenStreetMap Contributors https://www.openstreetmap.org

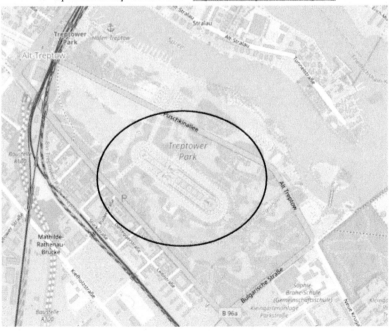

Soviet War Memorial in Tiergarten
OpenStreetMap Contributors https://www.openstreetmap.org

- **Day 5:** Climb the steps of the imposing Berlin Cathedral and admire its intricate architecture. Stroll down Unter den Linden – a historic boulevard lined with grand buildings – and end your day with a classical concert at the Philharmonie.

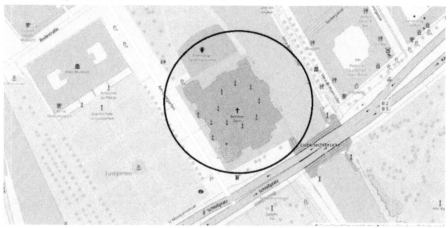

Berlin Cathedral off Schlossplatz
OpenStreetMap Contributors https://www.openstreetmap.org

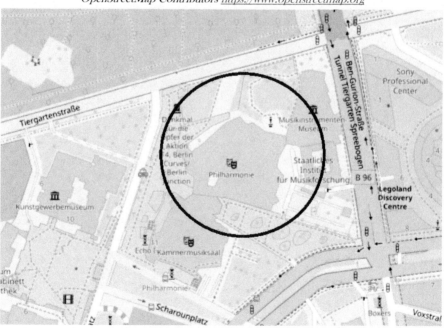

Philharmonie off Tiergartnestrasse
OpenStreetMap Contributors https://www.openstreetmap.org

For the Art Enthusiast: 4-Day Art Adventure

- **Day 1:** Start your day at Hamburger Bahnhof, a contemporary art powerhouse with a world-renowned collection. In the afternoon, explore the street art scene of Kreuzberg, where murals and installations adorn every corner.

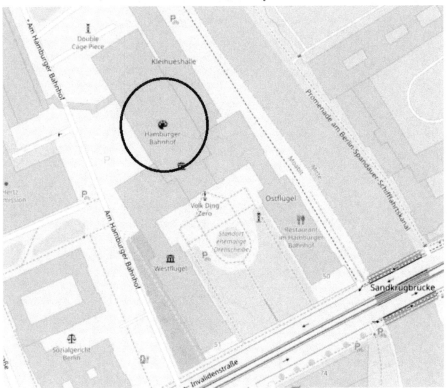

Hamburger Bahnhof off Invalidenstrasse, am Hamburger Banhof

OpenStreetMap Contributors https://www.openstreetmap.org

- **Day 2:** Discover Mitte's vibrant universe. Visit the Gemäldegalerie for a glimpse into European art history, and then uncover the experimental works at **KW** Institute for Contemporary Art.

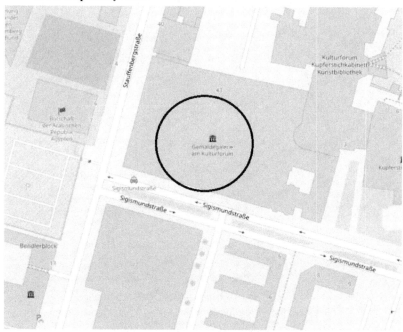

Gemäldegalerie off Sigismundstrasse
OpenStreetMap Contributors https://www.openstreetmap.org

KW Institute for Contemporary Art off Auguststrasse
OpenStreetMap Contributors https://www.openstreetmap.org

- **Day 3:** Stroll through the eclectic Friedrichshain neighborhood, discovering hidden galleries like Kunstquartier Bethanien and C/O Berlin. In the afternoon, wander through the trendy Hackescher Höfe, where art shops and cafes coexist in charming courtyards.

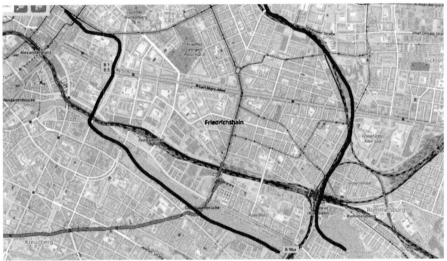

Friedrichshain neighborhood
OpenStreetMap Contributors https://www.openstreetmap.org

- **Day 4:** For a one-of-a-kind experience, visit the Urban Nation Art Museum, housed in a former brewery. In the evening, catch a performance at the Schaubühne am Lehniner Platz, a renowned theater known for its avant-garde productions.

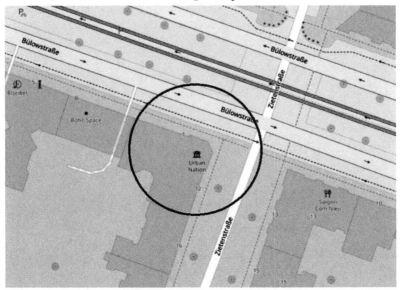

Urban Nation off Bulowstrasse
OpenStreetMap Contributors https://www.openstreetmap.org

Schaubühne am Lehniner Platz off Kurfurstendamm
OpenStreetMap Contributors https://www.openstreetmap.org

For the Foodie: 3-Day Culinary Saga

- **Day 1:** Embark on a culinary tour of Mitte, savoring traditional German fare at Zur Haxe or modern interpretations at Nobelhart & Schmutzig. In the afternoon, indulge in sweet treats at the iconic Marzipanfiguren Café or explore the international flavors of Hackescher Markt.

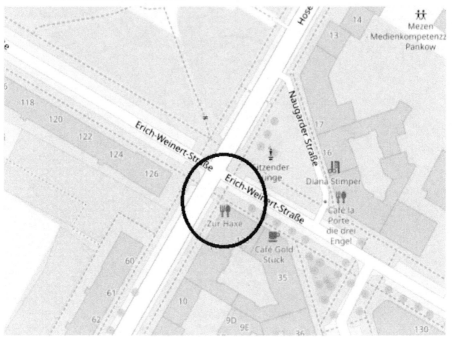

Zur Haxe restaurant off Erich-Weinert Strasse

OpenStreetMap Contributors https://www.openstreetmap.org

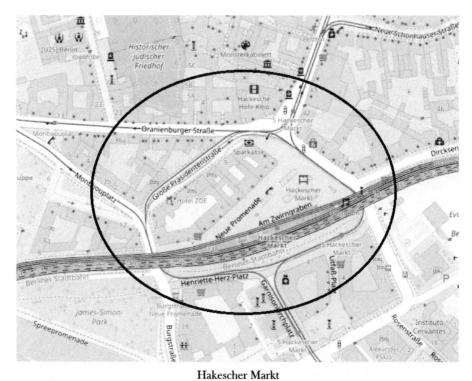

Hakescher Markt

OpenStreetMap Contributors https://www.openstreetmap.org

- **Day 2:** Venture into Prenzlauer Berg, a neighborhood known for its trendy cafes and innovative restaurants. Sample a delicious brunch at Distrikt Coffee or enjoy a hearty meal at Max und Moritz. In the evening, head to Kreuzberg for a lively atmosphere and diverse culinary options, from Turkish kebabs to Vietnamese pho.

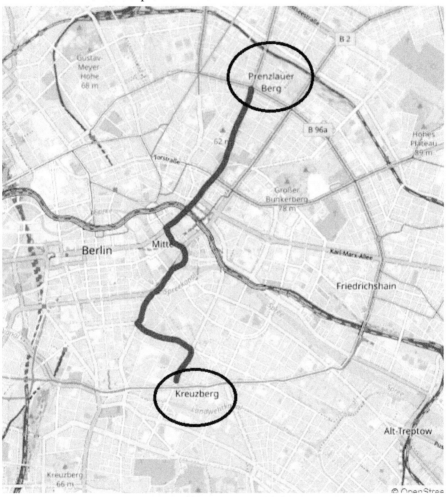

Make the trek from Prenzlauerberg to Kreuzberg for the full culinary experience.

OpenStreetMap Contributors https://www.openstreetmap.org

- **Day 3:** Take a street food tour in Neukölln, a melting pot of cultures reflected in its diverse food stalls. Sample Korean BBQ, Vietnamese bahn mi, or authentic Turkish gözleme. In the evening, explore the lively Simon-Dach-Straße, where bars and restaurants spill onto the street.

Bars and cafes galore in Simon-Dach Strasse, Kopernikisstrasse, Krossener Strasse, and Gruenberger Strasse

OpenStreetMap Contributors *https://www.openstreetmap.org*

For Families: 4-Day Family Fun

- **Day 1:** Start your day at LEGOLAND Discovery Centre, where kids can build, play, and explore. In the afternoon, take a boat trip on the Spree River, absorbing stunning views of the city.

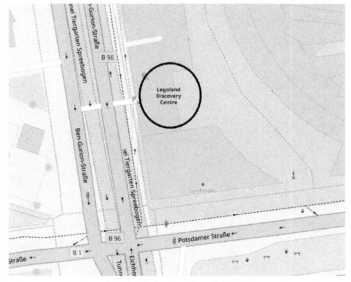

Build, explore, and enjoy LEGOland.

OpenStreetMap Contributors *https://www.openstreetmap.org*

- **Day 2:** Visit the Berlin Zoo, home to over 9,000 animals from around the world. In the afternoon, let loose at the Mauerpark flea market, searching for treasures and enjoying the lively atmosphere.

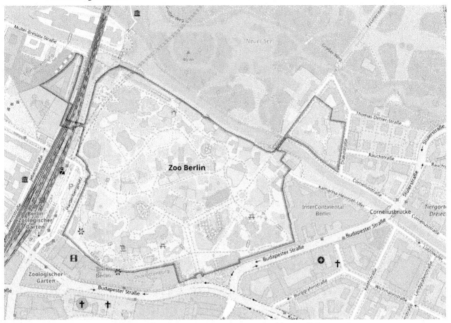

Enjoy an evening with the family at the Berlin Zoo.

OpenStreetMap Contributors https://www.openstreetmap.org

- **Day 3:** Take a trip to Tiergarten, a sprawling park perfect for picnics and outdoor activities. In the afternoon, visit the Natural History Museum, where dinosaurs and other fascinating creatures come to life.

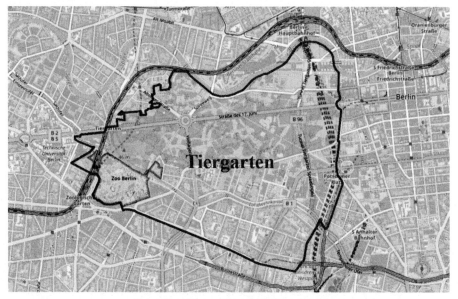

Enjoy the great outdoors with Tiergarten.

OpenStreetMap Contributors *https://www.openstreetmap.org*

- **Day 4:** Explore the interactive exhibits at the MACHmit! Museum for Children, where kids can learn through play and experimentation.

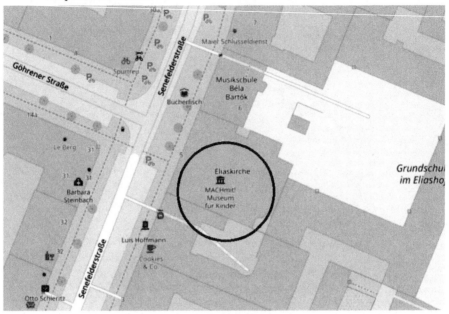

MACHmit! off Senefelderstrasse

OpenStreetMap Contributors https://www.openstreetmap.org

For the Night Owl: 3-Day after Dark Escapade

- **Day 1:** Kick off your evening with a cocktail at Monkey Bar, offering panoramic views of the city. Dive into the energetic nightlife of Friedrichshain, hopping between eclectic bars and underground clubs like Berghain or Matrix.

- **Day 2:** Explore the Kreuzberg nightlife scene, with its diverse music scene and laid-back vibes. Check out SO36 Club for punk gigs, or catch a techno DJ set at Club Gretchen.

- **Day 3:** Experience the alternative culture of Mitte. Enjoy drinks at the bohemian Prater Garten or dance the night away at Kit Kat Club, famous for its dazzling drag shows.

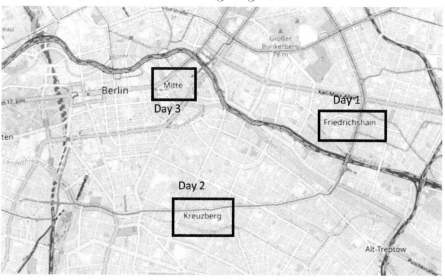

Enjoy the Berlin nightlife to the fullest.

OpenStreetMap Contributors https://www.openstreetmap.org

For the Thrill Seeker: 2-Day Adventure Spree

- **Day 1:** Go on a bike tour through Berlin's hidden alleys and historical landmarks, feeling the wind in your hair. For a higher adrenaline rush, climb the Fernsehturm, the tallest structure in Germany, for breathtaking views.

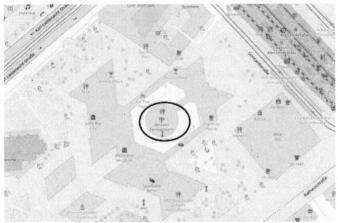

Take in the beautiful view of Berlin from the Fernsehturm.
OpenStreetMap Contributors https://www.openstreetmap.org

- **Day 2:** Paddle down the Spree River on a kayak tour, experiencing the city from a new angle. In the afternoon, challenge yourself at the high ropes course at MountMitte, testing your climbing skills.

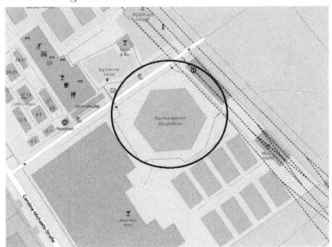

Test your climbing skills at MountMitte.
OpenStreetMap Contributors https://www.openstreetmap.org

For the Off-the-Beaten-Path Explorer: 5-Day Alternative Berlin

- **Day 1:** Discover the bohemian charm of Friedrichshain, exploring vintage shops and independent cafes. In the afternoon, visit the Computerspielemuseum, a nostalgic trip down memory lane for gamers.

- **Day 2:** Venture into Neukölln, a rapidly changing neighborhood with a multicultural vibe. Wander through the Columbiadamm area, known for its Turkish street food and markets.

- **Day 3:** Explore Wedding's artistic community, where industrial spaces have been transformed into studios and galleries. Visit the Mauerpark flea market on Sunday mornings for a treasure trove of vintage finds.

- **Day 4:** Take a walking tour of Lichtenberg, a historically significant district with Soviet-era architecture and hidden historical gems. In the evening, catch a concert at the Astra Kulturhaus, a renowned venue for alternative music.

- **Day 5:** Rent a bike and explore Prenzlauer Berg, Berlin, a sprawling green oasis with lakes, sculptures, and hidden memorials. In the afternoon, visit the Jewish Museum Berlin, a thought-provoking museum in Daniel Libeskind's striking architectural masterpiece.

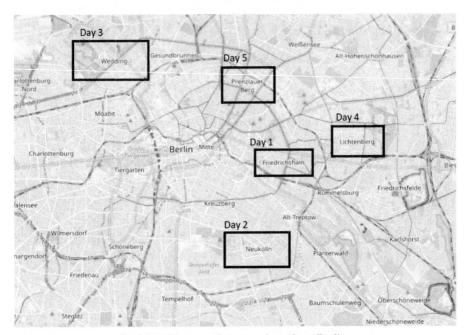

Explore off-beaten adventures throughout Berlin.

OpenStreetMap Contributors <u>*https://www.openstreetmap.org*</u>

These are mere starting points. Use these itineraries as inspiration to build your Berlin adventure, tailoring them to your interests and pace. Explore hidden alleys, stumble upon unexpected delights, and discover the real pulse of this dynamic city. Berlin awaits.

Chapter 11: Day Trips beyond the City

With its impeccable energy and rich history, Berlin is a captivating city. However, sometimes the call of the open road beckons. Step outside the city limits and discover a medley of landscapes, charming towns, and experiences waiting to be explored. This chapter unveils a selection of day trips, each offering a chance to discover German culture, connect with nature, or unwind in picturesque settings.

Potsdam.
https://www.pexels.com/photo/new-palace-by-pond-in-potsdam-germany-19019475/

For the History Buff

- **Potsdam:** Imagine another time of elegant living in Prussian grandeur at the UNESCO-listed Sanssouci Palace, Frederick the Great's summer retreat. Explore the Cecilienhof Palace, where the Potsdam Conference shaped the post-war world, and stroll through the Dutch Quarter's charming red-brick lanes.

- **Dresden:** Witness the architectural phoenix rising from the ashes – the Frauenkirche and Zwinger Palace. Wander through the restored Altstadt, marveling at the rebuilt Opera House and the Green Vault, brimming with exquisite treasures.

- **Oranienburg:** Pay your respects to the dark chapters of history at the Sachsenhausen Concentration Camp Memorial, then find solace in the landscaped gardens of Oranienburg Palace and serene Lehnitzsee Lake.

For the Nature Lover

- **Märkische Schweiz Nature Park:** Hike through the rolling hills and verdant forests of the Märkische Schweiz Biosphere Reserve. Discover the charming village of Buckow, explore the medieval Chorin Monastery, and learn about the region's rich history at the museum.

- **Barnim Nature Park:** Become absorbed in the Schorfheide-Chorin Biosphere Reserve. Paddle along the tranquil Werbellinsee Lake, spot diverse birdlife, and visit the impressive Chorin Monastery, a haven of peace amid the ancient forest.

- **Eberswalde:** This family-friendly haven beckons a delightful day at the Familiengarten Eberswalde. Explore the Eberswalde Zoo, where Central European wildlife comes alive, and enjoy a scenic walk along the Finow Canal.

For the Cultural Explorer

- **Brandenburg an der Havel:** Journey back through time in the medieval Brandenburg Cathedral. Drown yourself in the arts scene at the Brandenburger Theater and uncover history by the riverfront in the Brandenburger Old Town.

- **Saxony Switzerland National Park:** Embark on a breathtaking journey through the Elbe Sandstone Mountains. Hike through dramatic gorges, marvel at towering rock formations, and discover the region's flora and fauna.

- **Lübbenau in the Spreewald:** Glide through the enchanting Spreewald forest on a traditional punt, marveling at the network of canals and colorful houses. Explore the charming town of Lübbenau, known for its conventional Spreewald cuisine and folklore.

Planning Your Day Trip

- Consider your interests and preferences. History buffs will gravitate toward Potsdam and Dresden, while nature lovers will adore Märkische Schweiz and Barnim Nature Parks.

- Choose your mode of transportation. Trains and regional buses offer convenient access to most destinations. Renting a car provides flexibility but requires navigating unfamiliar roads.

- Pack appropriately for the weather and planned activities. Hiking boots and rain gear are essential for some destinations, while comfortable shoes suffice for others.

- Don't forget to research opening hours and ticket prices for attractions. Many museums offer discounts for students and seniors.

Bonus Tip: Explore the local markets and cafes in each destination. You'll find delicious regional specialties and souvenirs and connect with the friendly locals.

These day trips are only a taste of the offerings beyond Berlin. The surrounding region promises endless adventures with its rich history, stunning landscapes, and vibrant culture. Feel free to research further and tailor your day trip to your interests and preferences.

Bonus Chapter: Useful German Survival Phrases

Mastering essential German phrases will go a long way to navigating Berlin seamlessly. Don't worry if you're a beginner. This chapter equips you with the language tools to conquer everyday situations and engage with locals.

Greetings and Politeness

- **Guten Morgen** (Gooten Mawr-gen): Good morning (used until noon).
- **Guten Tag** (Gooten Tahg): Good day (used afternoon).
- **Hallo** (Hah-low): Hello (informal).
- **Grüß Gott** (Groos Got): Hello (used in Bavaria).
- **Auf Wiedersehen** (Owf Vee-der-zeen): Goodbye.
- **Bitte** (Bit-te): Please.
- **Danke** (Dahn-keh): Thank you.
- **Bitte Schön** (Bit-te shern): You're welcome.
- **Entschuldigung** (Ent-shool-dee-goong): Excuse me/Sorry.

Getting Around

- **Wo Ist** (Vo ist): Where is.
- **Die Toilette** (dee Toy-let-te): the toilet.
- **Der Bahnhof** (der Bahn-hohf): the train station.

- **Ein Taxi** (ayn Tahk-see): a taxi.
- **Können Sie Mir Bitte Helfen?** (Kuhn-en zee mir bit-te hel-fen): Can you please help me?
- **Wie Komme Ich Nach [Place Name]?** (Vee koh-meh ihk nahk...): How do I get to...?
- **Ein Ticket Nach [Place Name], Bitte.** (Ayn Tik-et nahk..., bit-te): One ticket to..., please.

Eating and Drinking

- **Guten Appetit!** (Goo-ten Ah-peh-teet): Enjoy your meal!
- **Ich Hätte Gerne...** (Ikh het-te gar-ne...): I would like...
- **Die Speisekarte, Bitte** (dee Shpay-ze-kar-te, bit-te): the menu, please.
- **Kann Ich Bitte [Dish Name] Haben?** (Kahn ikh bit-te... hah-ben): Can I have..., please?
- **Die Rechnung, Bitte.** (Dee rekh-nung, bit-te): The check, please.
- **Ein Bier, Bitte.** (Ayn Bee-er, bit-te): A beer, please.
- **Prost!** (Prohst): Cheers!

Shopping

- **Wie Viel Kostet Das?** (Vee feel koh-stet das): How much does this cost?
- **Kann Ich Das Anprobieren?** (Kahn ikh das an-probee-ren): Can I try this on?
- **Ich Nehme Das.** (Ikh nehme das): I'll take it.
- **Haben Sie Das In [Size/Color]?** (Hah-ben zee das in...): Do you have this in...?
- **Wo Finde Ich...?** (Vo fin-de ikh...): Where can I find...?

Emergencies

- **Hilfe!** (Heel-feh!): Help!
- **Feuer!** (Foy-er!): Fire!
- **Polizei!** (Po-lee-tsay!): Police!
- **Rufen Sie Die Polizei!** (Roo-fen zee dee Po-lee-tsay): Call the police!

- **Ich Brauche Einen Arzt.** (Ih brauch-e ay-nen Arst): I need a doctor.
- **Wo Ist Das Nächste Krankenhaus?** (Vo ist das neks-te Krahn-ken-haus): Where is the nearest hospital?

Bonus

- **Na Klar!** (Nah klaar): Of course!
- **Kein Problem.** (Kine Proh-blehm): No problem.
- **Lecker!** (Lek-ker): Delicious!
- **Viel Spaß!** (Feel Shpahss): Have fun!

Pronunciation Tips

- The "r" is usually rolled.
- The "ä" is similar to the "a" in "pace."
- The "ü" is similar to the "u" in "French."
- The "ch" is usually a voiceless velar fricative, like the "h" in "loch."

Remember, even a few basic phrases can go a long way in Berlin. Don't be afraid to make mistakes, and have fun exploring the language. Viel Glück (good luck) with your Berlin adventure.

Appendix

This appendix provides a quick reference guide to Berlin's diverse attractions, monuments, and museums, categorized alphabetically for your convenience. Please note that some attractions are outside the city center, so check the individual listings for more details.

A

- **Adlershofer Tor:** A triumphal arch marking the entrance to the former Treptower Park amusement park.
- **Alte Nationalgalerie:** Neoclassical museum housing a collection of 19th-century European art.
- **AquaDom:** Europe's largest cylindrical aquarium is in the Radisson Blu Hotel.

B

- **Bauhaus-Archiv:** Museum dedicated to the Bauhaus design movement.
- **Berlin Cathedral (Berliner Dom):** High Baroque cathedral with stunning views of the city.
- **Berlin Dungeon:** Interactive waxwork museum showcasing Berlin's dark history.
- **Berlin Philharmonic Orchestra:** Renowned orchestra performing at the Philharmonie concert hall.
- **Brandenburg Gate:** Iconic landmark symbolizing the unification of East and West Germany.

C

- **Checkpoint Charlie:** The former border crossing point between East and West Berlin is now a museum.

D

- **Deutsches Historisches Museum:** National museum tracing German history from the Middle Ages to the present.
- **DDR Museum:** Interactive museum showcasing everyday life in East Germany.

E

- **Einstein Tower:** Observatory designed by Albert Einstein.

F

- **Fernsehmuseum:** Museum dedicated to the history of television in Germany.
- **Fernsehturm:** Berlin's tallest structure, offering panoramic views from the observation deck.

G

- **Gemäldegalerie:** Museum housing a collection of European paintings from the 13th to the 19th centuries.
- **Gendarmenmarkt:** Square with three iconic buildings: the Konzerthaus, the Deutscher Dom, and the Französische Kirche.

H

- **Hamburger Bahnhof:** Museum of Contemporary Art.
- **Haus am Checkpoint Charlie:** Museum chronicling the attempts to escape from East Berlin.

I

- **Island of Museums (Museumsinsel):** A complex of five museums housing archaeological and cultural artifacts.

J

- **Jewish Museum:** The Museum documents Jewish history in Berlin.

K

- **Kaiser Wilhelm Memorial Church:** Ruined church left as a memorial to World War II.
- **Kulturforum:** Complex of museums and exhibition spaces.

L

- **LEGOLAND Discovery Center:** Interactive LEGO-themed attraction for children.

M

- **Märkisches Museum:** Museum of the History of Berlin and Brandenburg.
- **Memorial to the Murdered Jews of Europe:** Holocaust memorial with 2,711 concrete stelae.
- **Museum of Kommunikation:** Museum showcasing the history of communication technologies.

N

- **Neue Nationalgalerie:** Museum housing a collection of 20th-century art.

O

- **Olympiastadion:** Olympic Stadium, built for the 1936 Summer Olympics.

P

- **Pergamonmuseum:** Museum housing archaeological treasures from ancient Mesopotamia, Babylon, and Pergamon.
- **Potsdamer Platz:** Lively square with modern architecture and entertainment venues.

Q

- **Quadriga of Brandenburg Gate:** Bronze statue of Victoria, goddess of victory, atop the Brandenburg Gate.

R

- **Reichstag Building:** Seat of the German Parliament, offering tours and rooftop views.

S

- **Spy Museum:** Interactive museum exploring the world of espionage.
- **Sony Center:** Entertainment complex with theaters, restaurants, and the Berlin Philharmonic Orchestra.
- **Spreepark:** Abandoned amusement park with a quirky, post-apocalyptic atmosphere.

T

- **Tiergarten:** Large urban park with lakes, forests, and the Berlin Zoo.
- **Topography of Terror:** Museum documenting the history of the Gestapo and the SS.

U

- **U-Bahn:** Berlin's extensive underground railway system.

V

- **Victory Column:** Golden monument commemorating Prussian victories in the 19th century.

W

- **Wall Museum:** Museum showcasing the history and remnants of the Berlin Wall.
- **Willy Brandt House:** Museum dedicated to the life and work of former German Chancellor Willy Brandt.

Z

- **Zoologischer Garten Berlin:** One of Europe's largest zoos, with over 1,500 species.

If you enjoyed this book, a review on Amazon would be greatly appreciated because it would mean a lot to hear from you.

To leave a review:
1. Open your camera app.
2. Point your mobile device at the QR code.
3. The review page will appear in your web browser.

Thanks for your support!

Here's another book by Captivating Travels that you might like

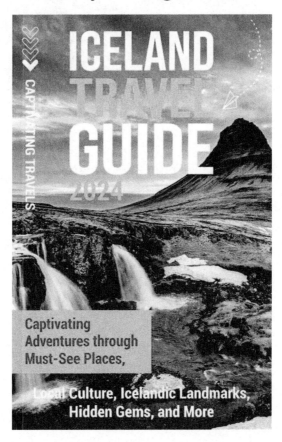

Welcome Aboard, Discover Your Limited-Time Free Bonus!

Hello, traveler! Welcome to the Captivating Travels family, and thanks for grabbing a copy of this book! Since you've chosen to join us on this journey, we'd like to offer you something special.

Check out the link below for a FREE Ultimate Travel Checklist eBook & Printable PDF to make your travel planning stress-free and enjoyable.

But that's not all - you'll also gain access to our exclusive email list with even more free e-books and insider travel tips. Well, what are you waiting for? Click the link below to join and embark on your next adventure with ease.

Access your bonus here:
https://livetolearn.lpages.co/checklist/
Or, Scan the QR code!

References

Amber. (2023, August 23). 10 Best Places to Visit in Berlin 2023 | Amber. Amberstudent.com. https://amberstudent.com/blog/post/top-10-tourist-attractions-in-berlin

Bisht, K. (2021, October 19). Top Places in Berlin for You to Experience the True Vibe of the Ancient City In 2022. Traveltriangle.com. https://traveltriangle.com/blog/places-to-visit-in-berlin/

Carney, T. (2022, January 25). The Best Places to Visit in Berlin, Germany. The Planet D: Adventure Travel Blog. https://theplanetd.com/places-to-visit-in-berlin/

Dearsley, B. (2000). 15 Top-Rated Tourist Attractions in Berlin | PlanetWare. Planetware.com. https://www.planetware.com/tourist-attractions-/berlin-d-bn-ber.htm

Editors, T. (2024, January 8). 25 Top Tourist Attractions in Berlin. Touropia. https://www.touropia.com/tourist-attractions-in-berlin/

Geary-Meyer, A. (2022, March 14). 16 Best Attractions in Berlin to Fill That Bucket List. Time out, Berlin. https://www.timeout.com/berlin/things-to-do/best-berlin-attractions

Lloyd. (2023, November 19). 17 Best Things to Do in Berlin, Germany. Hand Luggage Only. https://handluggageonly.co.uk/17-sights-you-need-to-see-on-a-first-time-visit-to-berlin-germany/

Maria. (2013). Berlin's Top 10 Attractions. Visitberlin.de; visitBerlin. https://www.visitberlin.de/en/berlins-top-10-attractions

U.S. News & World Report. (2020, July 29). 17 Best Things to Do in Berlin | U.S. News Travel. Usnews.com; U.S. News & World Report. https://travel.usnews.com/Berlin_Germany/Things_To_Do/

Zararia, P. Z. (2017, March 7). 21 Things to Do in Berlin. The Times of India. https://timesofindia.indiatimes.com/travel/things-to-do/21-things-to-do-in-berlin/articleshow/53319043.cms

Printed in Great Britain
by Amazon

47557026R00116